Women in the New Testament

Women in the New Testament

Catherine A. Cory
with Little Rock Scripture Study staff

LITURGICAL PRESS
Collegeville, Minnesota

littlerockscripture.org

Nihil obstat for the commentary text by Catherine A. Cory: Rev. Robert Harren, *Censor deputatus*
Imprimatur for the commentary text by Catherine A. Cory: ✠ Most Rev. Patrick M. Neary, C.S.C., Bishop of St. Cloud, August 9, 2023

Cover design by John Vineyard. Interior art by Ned Bustard. Photo and illustrations on pages 17, 18, 26, 37, 38, 54, 57, 65, 72, 73, 83, 86, 89, and 103 courtesy of Getty Images. Photo on page 109 courtesy of Yale University. Map on page 83 created by Robert Cronan of Lucidity Information Design, LLC.

 This symbol indicates material that was created by Little Rock Scripture Study to supplement the biblical text and commentary. Some of these inserts first appeared in the Little Rock Catholic Study Bible; others were created specifically for this book by Catherine A. Cory.

1   2   3   4   5   6   7   8   9

Library of Congress Cataloging-in-Publication Data

Names: Cory, Catherine A., author. | Little Rock Scripture Study Staff, author.
Title: Women in the New Testament / Catherine A. Cory ; with Little Rock Scripture Study staff.
Description: Collegeville, MN : Liturgical Press, [2024] | Series: Little Rock scripture study | Includes bibliographical references. | Summary: "In Women in the New Testament, Catherine Cory delves into the lives of the women who befriended Jesus, were healed and transformed by him, followed him as disciples, and proclaimed the good news of his resurrection. Commentary, study and reflection questions, prayers, and access to online lectures are included. 6 lessons"— Provided by publisher.
Identifiers: LCCN 2023030406 (print) | LCCN 2023030407 (ebook) | ISBN 9780814667569 (trade paperback) | ISBN 9780814667583 (epub)
Subjects: LCSH: Women in the Bible. | Bible. New Testament.
Classification: LCC BS575 .C585 2024 (print) | LCC BS575 (ebook) | DDC 220.9/2082—dc23/eng/20230808
LC record available at https://lccn.loc.gov/2023030406
LC ebook record available at https://lccn.loc.gov/2023030407

TABLE OF CONTENTS

 Wrap-Up Lectures and Discussion Tips for Facilitators are available for each lesson at no charge. Find them online at LittleRockScripture.org/Lectures/WomenNT.

Welcome

The Bible is at the heart of what it means to be a Christian. It is the Spirit-inspired word of God for us. It reveals to us the God who created, redeemed, and guides us still. It speaks to us personally and as a church. It forms the basis of our public liturgical life and our private prayer lives. It urges us to live worthily and justly, to love tenderly and wholeheartedly, and to be a part of building God's kingdom here on earth.

Though it was written a long time ago, in the context of a very different culture, the Bible is no relic of the past. Catholic biblical scholarship is among the best in the world, and in our time and place, we have unprecedented access to it. By making use of solid scholarship, we can discover much about the ancient culture and religious practices that shaped those who wrote the various books of the Bible. With these insights, and by praying with the words of Scripture, we allow the words and images to shape us as disciples. By sharing our journey of faithful listening to God's word with others, we have the opportunity to be stretched in our understanding and to form communities of love and learning. Ultimately, studying and praying with God's word deepens our relationship with Christ.

Women in the New Testament

The resource you hold in your hands is divided into six lessons. Each lesson involves personal prayer and study using this book and the experience of group prayer, discussion, and a wrap-up lecture.

If you are using this resource in the context of a small group, we suggest that you meet six times, discussing one lesson per meeting. Allow about 90 minutes for the small group gathering. Small groups function best with eight to twelve people to ensure good group dynamics and to allow all to participate as they wish.

Some groups choose to have an initial gathering before their regular sessions begin. This allows an opportunity to meet one another, pass out books, and, if desired, view the optional intro lecture for this study available on the "Resources" page of the Little Rock Scripture Study website (littlerockscripture.org).

Every Bible study group is a little bit different. Some of our groups like to break each lesson up into two weeks of study so they are reading less each week and have more time to discuss the questions together at their weekly gatherings. If your group wishes to do this, simply agree how much of each lesson will be read each week, and only answer the questions that correspond to the material you read. Wrap-up lectures can then be viewed at the end of every other meeting rather than at the end of every meeting. Of course, this will mean that your study will last longer, and your group will meet more times.

WHAT MATERIALS WILL YOU USE?

The materials in this book include:

- Scripture passages to be studied, using the New American Bible, Revised Edition as the translation.
- Commentary by Catherine A. Cory.
- Occasional inserts 🔥 highlighting elements of the Scripture passages being studied.
- Questions for study, reflection, and discussion at the end of each lesson.
- Opening and closing prayers for each lesson, as well as other prayer forms available in the closing pages of the book.

In addition, there are wrap-up lectures available for each lesson. Your group may choose to purchase a DVD containing these lectures or make use of the video lectures available online at no charge. The link to these free lectures is: LittleRockScripture.org/Lectures/WomenNT. Of course, if your group has access to qualified speakers, you may choose to have live presentations.

Each person will need a current translation of the Bible. We recommend the *Little Rock Catholic Study Bible*, which makes use of the New American Bible, Revised Edition. Other translations, such as the New Jerusalem Bible or the New Revised Standard Version: Catholic Edition, would also work well.

HOW WILL YOU USE THESE MATERIALS?

Prepare in advance

Using Lesson One as an example:

- Begin with a simple prayer like the one found on page 11.

- Read the assigned material for Lesson One (pages 12–26) so that you are prepared for the weekly small group session.

- Answer the questions, Exploring Lesson One, found at the end of the assigned reading, pages 27–29.

- Use the Closing Prayer on page 29 when you complete your study. This prayer may be used again when you meet with the group.

Meet with your small group

- After introductions and greetings, allow time for prayer (about 5 minutes) as you begin the group session. You may use the prayer on page 11 (also used by individuals in their preparation) or use a prayer of your choosing.

- Spend about 45–50 minutes discussing the responses to the questions that were prepared in advance. You may also develop your discussion further by responding to questions and interests that arise during the discussion and faith-sharing itself.

- Close the discussion and faith-sharing with prayer, about 5–10 minutes. You may use the Closing Prayer at the end of each lesson or one of your choosing at the end of the book. It is important to allow people to pray for personal and community needs and to give thanks for how God is moving in your lives.

- Listen to or view the wrap-up lecture associated with each lesson (about 15 minutes). You may watch the lecture online, use a DVD, or provide a live lecture by a qualified local speaker. View the lecture together at the end of the session or, if your group runs out of time, you may invite group members to watch the lecture on their own time after the discussion.

A note to individuals

- If you are using this resource for individual study, simply move at your own pace. Take as much time as you need to read, study, and pray with the material.

- If you would like to share this experience with others, consider inviting a friend or family member to join you for your next study. Even a small group of two or three provides an opportunity for fruitful dialog and faith-sharing!

Women in the New Testament

LESSON ONE

Introduction and Mary, Mother of Jesus

Begin your personal study and group discussion with a simple and sincere prayer such as:

Prayer

God of love and consolation, as we study the women of the New Testament, open our hearts and minds to appreciate the unique gifts they each brought to their faith communities. May their witness inspire us today to use the gifts we have received in service of your holy ones.

Read the Introduction and pages 12–26, Lesson One, highlighting what stands out to you.

Respond to the questions on pages 27–29, Exploring Lesson One.

The Closing Prayer on page 29 is for your personal use and may be used at the end of group discussion.

INTRODUCTION

In almost any online or brick-and-mortar store that sells religious books, you will find a multitude of resources for studying the Bible. However, you might not think to inquire about the author's approach to the resources they are offering. For example, some books or commentaries focus on Scripture as literature, while others take a more historical or theological approach. Some methods of interpretation work better than others, depending on the topic being investigated. If you know the specific approach of the author of your biblical resource, you will have a better understanding of the kinds of questions he or she will raise and try to answer.

 The Second Vatican Council's "Dogmatic Constitution on Divine Revelation" (*Dei Verbum*) describes Scripture as the Word of God in the words of human authors. Biblical scholars call this a ***contextualist approach*** to the interpretation of biblical texts because it acknowledges the author's social and historical context. The Catholic Church is not the only denomination that takes this approach. Others include the United Methodist Church, the Episcopal Church, and the Evangelical Lutheran Church of America, to name a few. In contrast, churches that are sometimes called "fundamentalist" take a *literalist approach* to the interpretation of Scripture.

The approach of this study falls under the general category of "historical critical methodologies." To clarify, the term "critical" does not mean that we will be *criticizing* the Bible. Rather, it means that we will be *analyzing* the biblical text to better understand what the human author, inspired by the Holy Spirit, was trying to communicate through his writing. Our guiding principle for the study of the Bible is that it is the Word of God in the words of human authors. But to understand what the human author was trying to say, we need to be attentive to what can be known about the history, cultural norms, and literary conventions of the time in which the author was writing.

Questions and Challenges

Because the topic of this study is women in the New Testament, we will want to learn as much as we can about the everyday lives of first-century Near Eastern women. For example, what do we know about their role in the family or about their place in the larger Greco-Roman society of their time? We might also want to know what it was like for first-century women and girls to live in highly patriarchal cultures and with little knowledge of the science and medicine that we take for granted today. Also, how do the community-centered (collectivist) cultures of the Bible differ from individual-centered (individualist) cultures like those of the modern Western world (e.g., North America and Western Europe), and how do these differences impact our understanding of New Testament stories about women like the mother of Jesus, the Samaritan woman, Mary and Martha (the sisters of Lazarus), or Mary Magdalene?

Many of these questions can be answered to some extent by studying the scholarly research that has been published in the last two decades or so. This commentary will provide a summary of recent scholarship where it is relevant. However, we also must be aware of the challenges that archaeologists and historians face in reconstructing women's history. The development of history is an ongoing process of gathering artifacts, formulating hypotheses, and interpreting the evidence. While ancient writings about the lives of Greco-Roman women do exist, their authors, mostly male, focused on the rich and famous women of the time, who constituted less than 2 percent of the population. We have relatively little evidence of the everyday lives of the rest of the female population of that time, and we would be remiss if we assumed that women's lives were the same in every place and under all conditions.

The term **"Near East"** is roughly equivalent to an area of western Asia once called the Levant. The modern countries that inhabit this space include Egypt, Saudi Arabia, the United Arab Emirates, Syria, Israel, Palestine, Lebanon, Jordan, Turkey, and parts of Iran and Iraq.

The term **"Greco-Roman"** refers to the intermingling of Greek and Roman cultures during the period of 332 BCE–642 CE. Alexander the Great's military campaigns, which began in Egypt in 332 BCE, extended as far as India before his death in 323 BCE. Along the way he imposed Greek language and culture throughout his empire. Later, when Rome conquered the Greek world in 31 BCE, it further expanded its empire but retained much of Greek culture.

To begin to orient ourselves to what we will encounter in these lessons about women in the New Testament, I want to briefly describe three aspects of first-century Mediterranean cultures that highlight how different their lives were from our lives today.

A Culture Focused on Community

Most of us who have grown up in the modern Western world are products of an individualist culture. We value the human person's ability to achieve, to stand out in a crowd, and to make one's own decisions. While there is value in independence and personal freedom, we have all seen how, taken to the extreme, cooperation and collaboration in an individualist culture are sometimes looked upon with suspicion, and partisanship and division can run rampant.

By way of contrast, collectivist cultures in the ancient world of the Bible (and in other parts of the world today) prioritize community much more than the needs and wishes of the individual. A person's identity is firmly grounded in relationships, and virtue is found in supporting the community, not in excelling beyond the expectations of the community, whether that be the family, the village, or the wider public. Collectivist cultures value collaboration, conformity, and maintaining harmony within families and communities. Imagine the upset that a belligerent teenager would cause in such a family situation!

Gender in the Ancient World

What does it mean to be a woman or a man? This is an active question in the Western world today. Without going into the complexities of our contemporary issues, it is helpful to know that questions surrounding gender and sexuality are not new. What is different are the answers that have been proposed. Scholars who study the concept of gender in the ancient Mediterranean world describe it in terms of a one-sex model. In doing so, they cite Aristotle (388–322 BCE), who wrote, "The female is as it were a deformed male" (*Generation of animals* 2.3). In practical terms, this means that women and others who displayed feminine attributes were considered fundamentally inferior to men. However, much as it is today, wealthy women and women of high social status could wield much more power and influence in the public realm than women of modest means—and certainly more than people who were on the margins of society.

Honor and Shame

Another concept that is difficult for many modern readers of the Bible to understand is the notion of honor and shame. People who grow up in individualist cultures tend to think of honor and shame in terms of right and wrong, innocence and guilt, but people who are products of collectivist cultures think in terms of society's expectations of what promotes harmony in community and what disrupts the fabric of life. Modern Western cultures give priority to the rule of law and individual discernment of conscience, but ancient Eastern Mediterranean cultures focused more on behavior that was visible to others and that promoted strong relationships among family and community. Honor is a limited good in a collectivist culture. If someone challenges your honor, you need to respond lest you bring even more shame on yourself and your family.

We may struggle a bit to fully understand and appreciate these cultural realities because they are so different from what we are used to. But we will find our efforts entirely worthwhile as we begin to investigate the stories of women in the New Testament.

Note: Each of the six lessons in this study include suggestions for additional reading or activities that you might like to do on your own or with friends or members of your Bible study group. You will find these suggestions at the end of the book in the "For Further Investigation" section, organized by lesson. Enjoy!

historical details matters much less than the theological messages they convey.

The Gospels ("good news") are historical, but they are not history or biography in the modern sense. Rather, they are proclamations of faith in Jesus Christ embraced by early Christian communities. All **four Gospels** were written at least a generation after the death and resurrection of Jesus. Scholars typically date them as follows: Mark (70 CE or a few years earlier), Matthew and Luke (80–90 CE), and John (90–100 CE). We do not know a great deal about the authors of these Gospels, but in honor of the tradition, we will refer to them by the names assigned to each Gospel in the second century.

MARY, MOTHER OF JESUS

In this lesson, we will examine the New Testament Gospel stories about Mary, the mother of Jesus. Mary has been the subject of great devotion throughout the centuries, especially among Catholic Christians, and is even regarded as an intercessor before God for sinful humanity. However, the New Testament Gospels tell us very little about Mary. Hopefully, with the benefit of greater understanding of the cultural world of the New Testament, we can gain some new insights into Mary's life as the mother of Jesus and enrich our own appreciation of Mary as the mother of us all.

Among the New Testament texts, only the Gospels of Matthew and Luke tell the story of Jesus' conception and birth. These two Gospels were written at approximately the same time, circa 85 CE. Thus, they are not eyewitness accounts of the life of Jesus, who was likely born sometime between 6 and 4 BCE. Instead, Matthew and Luke were collectors of traditional stories and teachings by and about Jesus. They edited these materials to create a proclamation of faith, in story form, about Jesus as the Christ, the Son of the living God. We will encounter significant variations in the way their two accounts are told, but the accuracy of the

Mary, Mother of Jesus, in Matthew's Gospel

We will begin with Matthew's version of the stories associated with Mary's pregnancy and delivery of the child Jesus since Matthew's Gospel account is the sparest in the details it provides about Mary. Nevertheless, the section of this Gospel that we call the "infancy narratives" is long (Matt 1:1–2:23). Only the excerpts that refer to Mary will be included in this study, so you might want to use your Bible to read Matthew's infancy narratives in full.

As you read Matthew 1:18-25, notice how little we see of Mary in the story of Jesus' conception. In fact, Joseph and the angel are the main characters. We learn only that the woman who will be the mother of Jesus is named Mary and that she is betrothed to a man named Joseph. We are not told who her parents are, nor do we know where she is from. It is as if she is chosen from the anonymous masses of people in Roman Palestine to take the stage for a brief moment in this salvation story, only to quickly disappear again after the infancy scenes are completed.

15

Matthew 1:18-25

The Birth of Jesus. [18]Now this is how the birth of Jesus Christ came about. When his mother Mary was betrothed to Joseph, but before they lived together, she was found with child through the holy Spirit. [19]Joseph her husband, since he was a righteous man, yet unwilling to expose her to shame, decided to divorce her quietly. [20]Such was his intention when, behold, the angel of the Lord appeared to him in a dream and said, "Joseph, son of David, do not be afraid to take Mary your wife into your home. For it is through the holy Spirit that this child has been conceived in her. [21]She will bear a son and you are to name him Jesus, because he will save his people from their sins." [22]All this took place to fulfill what the Lord had said through the prophet:

[23]"Behold, the virgin shall be with child and
    bear a son,
    and they shall name him Emmanuel,"

which means "God is with us." [24]When Joseph awoke, he did as the angel of the Lord had commanded him and took his wife into his home. [25]He had no relations with her until she bore a son, and he named him Jesus.

In the first-century Eastern Mediterranean world, marriages were arranged and were principally about protecting family possessions and producing sons for the next generation of life. Fathers would decide on the arrangements of betrothal when their daughters were as young as ten to twelve years of age, but the marriage itself did not take place until after the girl entered her menarche (the beginning of menstruation), at which time she would be transferred from her father's home to the home of her husband and his family.

If the families were well-off and had good connections, the preparations and feasting associated with the wedding could last a full week. For those who were less fortunate, the wedding might have been limited to three or four days, but the entire village still would have been invited since villages were formed around extended family ties. Thus, large public events like weddings were occasions for reinforcing a family's honor status within the community. Of course, the flip side of this, as we see in this Gospel, was that a wedding could also be fraught with dangers resulting in a loss of family honor.

Mary's pregnancy before the consummation of her marriage is perhaps the worst thing that her family could imagine. Even if a woman was

Women in Matthew's Genealogy

The Gospel of Matthew opens with a genealogy of Jesus, starting with Abraham and moving through David and the Babylonian Exile until it reaches Mary, the mother of Jesus (1:1-17).

Unlike modern genealogies that attempt to establish one's biological origins, ancient genealogies establish the status of the one whose genealogy is set forth and hint at the child's destiny. For example, Matthew's genealogy presents Jesus as a descendant of Abraham (the father of Judaism) and as a king much greater than David. By contrast, Luke begins his genealogy with Joseph, the supposed father of Jesus, and ends with Adam, the son of God (3:23-38).

Luke does not include any women in his genealogy of Jesus, but Matthew includes five, all of whom were marginalized as outsiders in some way, but without whom Jesus could not have been born: **Tamar**, a Canaanite woman and daughter-in-law of Judah, son of Jacob (Gen 38); **Rahab**, a Gentile prostitute who protected Joshua's scouts as they prepared to enter the Promised Land (Josh 2); **Ruth**, the Moabite daughter-in-law of Naomi, who was the great-great-grandmother of David (Ruth 1); **"the wife of Uriah,"** whose name was Bathsheba, whom David took into his harem after having her husband killed in battle (2 Sam 11); and **Mary**, the mother of Jesus. Their stories are very interesting!

raped, she was considered "damaged goods" and no longer suitable for an honorable marriage. This is why Joseph struggles over how to proceed with his wedding prior to receiving the angel's message. The narrator of the story describes Joseph as a righteous man, meaning that he knows what his culture expects and has been known to act accordingly. In this case, Joseph would be expected to publicly divorce Mary, but instead he proceeds with the marriage, suggesting (wrongly) to their neighbors that he is not as righteous as everyone thinks! For Mary, an unmarried pregnant girl of fourteen or fifteen years of age, there is little to be done to restore her honor in the eyes of their neighbors. How will she cope?

Mary is again mentioned briefly in Matthew's story of the visit of the magi, who are not kings but rather scholars of the esoteric sciences, such as astrology and dream interpretation. The narrator explains how these scholars are following the star of "the newborn king of the Jews" (Matt 2:2). Their first stop is Jerusalem, where they inquire about where they might find this baby king. Of course, this visit from outsiders seeking a king causes great consternation in Herod the Great's court. Herod clearly perceives this child's very existence to be a threat to his own status as king. The irony of the situation is that Herod is himself a Jew.

In consultation with the chief priests and scribes of the Jerusalem temple, Herod discovers that the messiah is to be born in Bethlehem, a distance of approximately 9 kilometers (5.5 miles) from Jerusalem. Herod gives this information to the magi under the false pretense that he wants to worship the newborn king.

In the following passage, the magi arrive in Bethlehem:

Matthew 2:9-12

[9]After their audience with the king they set out. And behold, the star that they had seen at its rising preceded them, until it came and stopped over the place where the child was. [10]They were overjoyed at seeing the star, [11]and on entering the house they saw the child with Mary his mother. They prostrated themselves and did him homage. Then they opened their treasures and offered him gifts of gold, frankincense, and myrrh. [12]And having been warned in a dream not to return to Herod, they departed for their country by another way.

Note that we are told nothing about Mary in this story except that she is present with her child when the magi arrive to meet him. She is not given any words to speak, and no actions are attributed to her. Even when these visitors from a strange land provide her child with gifts befitting a person of lofty social status, such as a king or deity, the narrator tells us nothing about her reaction. It is up to us to imagine, if we can, what Mary is thinking and feeling as this story unfolds. Is she fearful? Curious? What sustains her?

Today's Christians tend to think of the first Christmas as a beautifully peaceful and tender experience for Mary and Joseph, but as this Gospel writer tells this next story, it was far from tranquil. It was dangerous! Matthew describes how this little family became refugees in an effort to save their own lives:

Matthew 2:13-15

The Flight to Egypt. [13]When they had departed, behold, the angel of the Lord appeared to Joseph in a dream and said, "Rise, take the child and his mother, flee to Egypt, and stay there until I tell you. Herod is going to search for the child to destroy him." [14]Joseph rose and took the child and his mother by night and departed for Egypt. [15]He stayed there until the death of Herod, that what the Lord had said through the prophet might be fulfilled, "Out of Egypt I called my son."

Matthew's description of the departure to Egypt and the eventual return "[o]ut of Egypt" is highly symbolic, designed to show Jesus as the new Moses. However, the storyline is also significant insofar as it reminds us that refugee immigration is not a new reality. Like today, these ancient journeys were perilous. Most people traveled on foot and by caravan, but not at night, as Joseph and Mary do (2:14). Nighttime travel was extremely dangerous because of bandits and other unseemly characters patrolling the roads. Ancients also believed that demons or evil spirits were especially active at

Engraving of the flight to Egypt by Julius Schnorr von Carolsfeld (1794-1872)

night (e.g., see Ps 91:5-6). When the Gospel notes that Joseph took mother and child and disappeared into the night, it is painting a picture of the terror that this young family was facing.

Mary is mentioned only a few other times in Matthew's Gospel. The first is in Jesus' genealogy, where she is the last of five extraordinary women without whom his family tree would not be complete (1:16). At another point in the Gospel, Mary is unnamed but is described as Jesus' mother (12:46-47; cf. Mark 3:31-32). A final reference is made in the context of the people of Nazareth trying to identify Jesus. They call him "the carpenter's son" and name Mary as his mother (13:55; cf. Mark 6:3). Ordinarily a person would have been identified with reference to the father alone.

Mary, Mother of Jesus, in Luke's Gospel

Luke tells a rather different story about the conception and birth of Jesus. Remember that neither Gospel writer was an eyewitness to the birth and early childhood of Jesus. Moreover, although ancient birth stories might have included some basic historical information, like where the person was born or the identity of their parents, they were not history or biography in the way that we understand these terms today. Rather, the primary function of ancient infancy narratives was to convey a message about the person's importance to society or what that person's destiny would be. In the case of Luke's Gospel, the conception and birth of Jesus marks a decisive transition from a period of promise to the time of fulfillment in the great salvation story, the coming reign of God.

Luke's Gospel begins with the parallel and interlaced stories of the conception and birth of John the Baptist and the conception and birth of Jesus (Luke 1–2). First, we encounter Zechariah and Elizabeth, the soon-to-be parents of John the Baptist (1:5-25). Zechariah is described as a priest in the service of the Jerusalem temple. Elizabeth, also regarded as a righteous person—though here "righteousness" is clearly linked with obedience to God's law (see 1:6)—is elderly and without any children. In other words, her status is uncertain when it comes to the issue of honor and shame because she has not been able to fulfill society's expectation that she provide her husband with a male heir. When Zechariah is about to fulfill his duty of making the incense offering in the temple, an angel appears and tells him that his wife will have a son and that they should name him John. The angel also describes this child's role in God's plan of salvation as a prophet in the spirit of Elijah (see Mal 3:1-2, 23-24). Zechariah asks, "How shall I know this?" (1:18), and the angel's response is the sign that God's word will be fulfilled.

This account follows the standard literary pattern of ancient birth narratives in Scripture (the announcement of birth is made by an angel; the name and destiny of the child is given; some objection or protest is made; a sign or confirmation is given by the angel; an account of the birth follows; see also Gen 17 and Judg 13). Typically, the women in these accounts are not expected to conceive for a variety of reasons (they are too old, too young, not married, etc.).

Luke uses this same pattern to describe the conception and birth of Jesus. However, instead of featuring a male of the priestly order in Jerusalem as the central character (as in John's birth narrative), he features a woman from a small town in Galilee:

Luke 1:26-38

Announcement of the Birth of Jesus. [26]In the sixth month, the angel Gabriel was sent from God to a town of Galilee called Nazareth, [27]to a virgin betrothed to a man named Joseph, of the house of David, and the virgin's name was Mary. [28]And coming to her, he said, "Hail, favored one! The Lord is with you." [29]But she was greatly troubled at what was said and pondered what sort of greeting this might be. [30]Then the angel said to her, "Do not be afraid, Mary, for you have found favor with God. [31]Behold, you will conceive in your womb and bear a son, and you shall name him Jesus. [32]He will be great and will be called Son of the Most High, and the Lord God will give him the throne of David his father, [33]and he will rule over the house of Jacob forever, and of his kingdom there will be no end." [34]But Mary said to the angel, "How can this be, since I have no relations with a man?" [35]And the angel said to her in reply, "The holy Spirit will come upon you, and the power of the Most High will overshadow you. Therefore the child to be born will be called holy, the Son of God. [36]And behold, Elizabeth, your relative, has also conceived a son in her old age, and this is the sixth month for her who was called barren; [37]for nothing will be impossible for God." [38]Mary said, "Behold, I am the handmaid of the Lord. May it be done to me according to your word." Then the angel departed from her.

In terms of form, many of the elements of this story are like those found in the story of Zechariah and even appear in the same order. The soon-to-be mother (Mary) and guardian of Jesus (Joseph) are identified. The angel Gabriel appears to Mary and calls her favored before God. He tells her that she will have a son and that he should be named Jesus. The angel also describes this child's role in God's plan of salvation as the long-awaited king in the line of David. Mary asks, "How can this be?" (1:34), and the angel's response is the sign that God's word will be fulfilled.

But here is where the two stories diverge. When Zechariah asks, "How shall I know this?" (1:18), he is made mute until the time when God's message, as delivered by the angel, is fulfilled. This is not so much a punishment as it is a symbolic pause that makes way for a shift from a time of promise to the time of the realization of God's coming kingdom. In this sense, John's birth is seen as a fulfillment of Malachi 3:23-24, in which God announces the return of Elijah before the "day of the Lord." But when Mary asks, "How can this be?" and the angel describes Jesus' conception by the Holy Spirit, she says, "Behold, I am the handmaid of the Lord. May it be done to me according to your word" (1:38). Thus, Mary becomes a model of ready faith and humble servitude.

As an aside, you might want to investigate medieval and Renaissance artistic renditions of this Gospel story, which we call the Annunciation. You will see that they portray Mary as the fragile and passive mother of Jesus, but you might ask yourself whether these artists' portrayals describe what Mary was really like. How do you imagine Mary in this moment?

Luke's story of Mary, the mother of Jesus, is closely intertwined with his story of Elizabeth, the mother of John the Baptist, especially as he describes Mary's visit to Elizabeth, her cousin:

Luke 1:39-45

Mary Visits Elizabeth. [39]During those days Mary set out and traveled to the hill country in haste to a town of Judah, [40]where she entered the house of Zechariah and greeted Elizabeth. [41]When Elizabeth heard Mary's greeting, the infant leaped in her womb, and Elizabeth, filled with the holy Spirit, [42]cried out in a loud voice and said, "Most blessed are you among women, and blessed is the fruit of your womb. [43]And how does this happen to me, that the mother of my Lord should come to me? [44]For at the moment the sound of your greeting reached my ears, the infant in my womb leaped for joy. [45]Blessed are you who believed that what was spoken to you by the Lord would be fulfilled."

In our modern Western cultural mindset, we might imagine a newly pregnant Jewish woman hopping on a bus or into her car and making the trip—more than eighty miles—by herself to visit her elder cousin Elizabeth. But the initial readers of this Gospel story would have imagined a very different scenario: a young betrothed or newly married teenager making an extremely dangerous journey on foot over the period of several days, probably as part of a caravan of travelers and almost certainly with a male guardian lest she be raped and killed along the way. Ancients believed that protective amulets bearing the image of a powerful god or goddess could ward off evil spirits. Perhaps Luke believed that the divinely begotten child in Mary's womb protected her from danger.

Another important aspect of this story is the way that Luke invites readers to eavesdrop on "women's talk." In the first-century Mediterranean world, conversation about a woman's pregnancy and the baby in utero was a strictly private matter, not to be shared in a public setting. But here we get to observe these two pregnant mothers as they break out in praise of God for being chosen to participate in such a generative way in God's salvation story.

This image of a tender embrace between two cousins—one too old to bear a child and another pregnant before her time—was another popular subject of artists of the medieval and Renaissance periods in Europe. Today, it is commonly known as the Visitation.

Mary's response to Elizabeth's greeting, now known as the *Magnificat* (Luke 1:46-55), is a stunningly beautiful prayer in praise of God's ability to raise up the lowly and bring down the mighty, a theme that appears regularly in Luke's Gospel. It begins with allusions to the removal of shame from these two women, but it soon extends to a much wider audience: the poor and vulnerable whose shame will be lifted in God's coming kingdom. This prayer of praise has strong resonances with Hannah's prayer of praise, spoken after God removed Hannah's shame by giving her a son named Samuel (see 1 Sam 2:1-10). Later, Samuel would be the one to anoint David as king of Israel.

> ### Luke 1:46-56
>
> **The Canticle of Mary.** ⁴⁶And Mary said:
>
> "My soul proclaims the greatness of the Lord;
> ⁴⁷my spirit rejoices in God my savior.
> ⁴⁸For he has looked upon his handmaid's
> lowliness;
> behold, from now on will all ages call me
> blessed.
> ⁴⁹The Mighty One has done great things
> for me,
> and holy is his name.
> ⁵⁰His mercy is from age to age
> to those who fear him.
> ⁵¹He has shown might with his arm,
> dispersed the arrogant of mind and heart.
> ⁵²He has thrown down the rulers from their
> thrones
> but lifted up the lowly.
> ⁵³The hungry he has filled with good things;
> the rich he has sent away empty.
> ⁵⁴He has helped Israel his servant,
> remembering his mercy,
> ⁵⁵according to his promise to our fathers,
> to Abraham and to his descendants
> forever."
>
> ⁵⁶Mary remained with her about three months
> and then returned to her home.

Luke's Gospel includes four additional stories that involve the childhood of Jesus and that mention his mother at least briefly. The first is the story of Jesus' birth (Luke 2:1-7), in which Joseph is described as taking his betrothed, Mary, to Bethlehem so that they could be enrolled in a worldwide census and counted as belonging to the house of David. Historians have not been able to establish as fact that Caesar Augustus issued such a census, but Luke uses it as a way to locate Jesus' birth in Bethlehem, likely reflecting a much older tradition shared by Matthew's Gospel that the long-awaited messiah would come from Bethlehem, the hometown of King David.

Mary is described as wrapping the baby Jesus in "swaddling clothes" or "bands of cloth" (NRSV). Swaddling was an ancient custom that may have been practiced in hopes of ensuring a strong, healthy spine. Interestingly, this custom extended well into Europe's early modern period and even into contemporary practice in many places around the world.

Further, Luke describes Mary as placing the baby "in a manger, because there was no room for them in the inn" (2:7). Again, our modern Western mindset might cause us to think of these parents as making a request at the front desk of a local hotel for a crib to be brought to their room, but the situation in first-century Palestine would have been quite different. Most ordinary people's homes were divided into two areas: one side for the people and household activities and the other side for their animals. The human living quarters typically consisted of a single room (the ancient version of an open floor plan, but much, much smaller!), though some might have had an extra space that could be used as a guest sleeping place or a dining area.

The Greek word for this extra sleeping or dining space in a home is *kataluma*, which can be translated as "inn," though it was nothing like our modern inns. When a caravan of travelers came to town, people would open their guest spaces to visitors, but apparently, at least as Luke tells it, the one Mary and Joseph inquired about was already in use, presumably by folks of higher social status than they were. The manger was a feeding trough for the animals. Perhaps Luke envisioned that Mary would have more privacy giving birth among the animals than in the rest of the house, but the main point is that Mary and Joseph are ordinary Jews of limited means who have to make do with what is available to them.

The second of these additional stories about Jesus' childhood has to do with the shepherds who come to visit the baby Jesus at the prompting of an angel who tells them to go to Bethlehem to see the newborn messiah (2:8-20). Shepherding was one of several occupations reserved for the lowest classes of people, those who had little honor because they were nomadic or considered ritually unclean. Yet, in Luke's Gospel, shepherds are the ones chosen to witness to Jesus' honor status, which is publicly proclaimed in the angels' description of Jesus as "savior," "Messiah," and "Lord" (2:11) as well as in their song of praise: "Glory to God in the highest / and on earth peace to those on whom his favor rests" (2:14). As we have seen before, Mary plays a very limited role in this scene. We learn only that she "kept all these things, reflecting on them in her heart" (2:19). Alternatively, this sentence could be translated as "Mary treasured up all these words, bringing them together in her heart" (my translation).

The third story is the presentation in the temple (Luke 2:22-38). Luke's account is ambiguous about who is being purified (see 2:22), but some of its details reflect the regulations described in Leviticus 12:1-8, where we are told that a woman was considered ritually unclean for seven days after the birth of a male child, the same length of time as for her monthly period. On the eighth day, the newborn boy was circumcised, but the mother had to wait another thirty-three days before she could complete the time of her purification. This was done with a sacrificial offering of a year-old lamb and a young dove or pigeon, after which time she was declared "clean again after her flow of blood" (Lev 12:7). If she gave birth to a female child, the times of uncleanness were doubled. If the woman was too poor to afford the prescribed offering, she could bring two young pigeons or doves for the offering instead. Such is Luke's understanding of the economic status of Joseph and Mary's family.

Luke notes that two elders, Simeon and Anna, are present in the temple that day. Each speaks about Jesus' destiny, but Simeon also addresses Mary, saying, "[Y]ou yourself a sword will pierce" (2:35). This warning is probably a reference to a double-edged sword of discernment like the one mentioned in Ezekiel 14:17 (see also Rev 1:16), in which some receive

judgment and others are spared based on their faithfulness. Luke is not suggesting that Mary will be punished but that even Mary's faith will be tested as she struggles with her understanding of Jesus' destiny. She is not privileged in that regard.

Anna is only mentioned once in the New Testament (Luke 2:36-38). But pay close attention to what Luke says about her. She is a prophetess, a faithful wife, a devout widow of many years, who night and day prayed and fasted in the temple. Reflect on Anna as a model of the contemplative life. What does she teach us about orienting ourselves toward prayer in our daily lives?

Luke's fourth story about Jesus' childhood has to do with his finding in the temple. As you probably know, this is the fifth of the Joyful Mysteries of the rosary, which has been a favorite devotion of Catholics since the thirteenth century. All five Joyful Mysteries have their origin in Luke's Gospel:

1. The Annunciation (1:26-38)

2. The Visitation (1:39-45)

3. The Birth of Jesus (2:1-14)

4. The Presentation in the Temple (2:22-38)

5. The Finding in the Temple (2:41-51)

In this story, Luke presents Mary and Joseph as devout Jews who observe Jewish laws and participate in the religious practices of Judaism. In this case, they are making the annual pilgrimage to Jerusalem for Passover. The distance of approximately sixty-five miles would have taken several days to complete on foot. The Holy Family likely would have traveled in a caravan with other family members and friends going from Nazareth to Jerusalem for the same purpose.

Luke 2:41-51

The Boy Jesus in the Temple. [41]Each year his parents went to Jerusalem for the feast of Passover, [42]and when he was twelve years old, they went up according to festival custom. [43]After they had completed its days, as they were returning, the boy Jesus remained behind in Jerusalem, but his parents did not know it. [44]Thinking that he was in the caravan, they journeyed for a day and looked for him among their relatives and acquaintances, [45]but not finding him, they returned to Jerusalem to look for him. [46]After three days they found him in the temple, sitting in the midst of the teachers, listening to them and asking them questions, [47]and all who heard him were astounded at his understanding and his answers. [48]When his parents saw him, they were astonished, and his mother said to him, "Son, why have you done this to us? Your father and I have been looking for you with great anxiety." [49]And he said to them, "Why were you looking for me? Did you not know that I must be in my Father's house?" [50]But they did not understand what he said to them. [51]He went down with them and came to Nazareth, and was obedient to them; and his mother kept all these things in her heart.

panic and shock (Greek *ekplésso*). Hence Mary's words: "Son, why have you done this to us?" (2:48). The Greek word translated in the same verse as "with great anxiety" can also be translated as "distressing or torturing oneself." Her expression of shock after finally finding their son makes Jesus' response all the more striking. In the ancient Mediterranean world, his words would have carried the tone of an adult male talking down to a female in public. What might Mary be thinking? Would she also be grieving how quickly her son went from boyhood to manhood? Even so, the Gospel is careful to note that Jesus responds with obedience to his parents, even as Mary continues to struggle to discern what her son is destined to be.

The word **"rosary"** derives from the Latin word *rosarium*, which means "a rose garden" or "a garland of roses." As an aid to meditation, each decade (set of ten prayers) is associated with an event from the life of Jesus or Mary. Tradition associates the origin of the rosary with Saint Dominic in the thirteenth century. However, various versions of beads-on-a-cord used to count prayers were already in use as early as the ninth century.

At the start of this story, Luke notes that Jesus was twelve years old. We do not know whether the author intended this reference to be taken literally. In the first century, a boy of twelve was nearly a man—many were married by age fifteen—but the number twelve also represented fullness or completion in Jewish tradition.

After a full day of looking for Jesus among the caravan, Mary and Joseph leave their fellow travelers and return to Jerusalem to continue their search. Finally, after three days, they find him in the temple talking with the religious leaders, who have been thrown into wonderment (Greek *existémi*) over his answers. But his parents, upon seeing him, are struck with

Luke does not refer to Mary again until chapter 11. There, Jesus is described as teaching the people, and a woman calls out, "Blessed is the womb that carried you and the breasts at which you nursed," and Jesus replies, "Rather, blessed are those who hear the word of God and observe it" (11:27-28). What an astonishing statement— Jesus is asserting that those who listen to his words and act on them are even more blessed than his mother! The point here is not so much about Mary's blessedness, which has already been well established in this Gospel. Rather, what is most astonishing about Jesus' statement is that he prioritizes the extraordinary commitment of discipleship even over natural family relationships (see also Luke 8:19-21; 9:57-62).

Mary, Mother of Jesus, in the Acts of the Apostles

Outside of the Gospels of the New Testament, Mary is mentioned very briefly in the Acts of the Apostles, which is attributed to the Gospel writer Luke and was written sometime shortly after 70 CE. This book tells the story of the growth of the early church from the time of the ascension of the risen Christ into heaven, which is where Luke's Gospel ends, to the time of Paul's arrival in Rome after his arrest but before his martyrdom. At the end of Luke's story of the ascension, the apostles are told to wait in Jerusalem for "the promise of the Father," their baptism "with the holy Spirit" (Acts 1:4-5). Before pivoting to a narrative about appointing someone to take Judas's place among the Twelve, Luke provides this summary description of the early Christian community gathered in Jerusalem:

Acts 1:13-14

The First Community in Jerusalem. [13]When they entered the city they went to the upper room where they were staying, Peter and John and James and Andrew, Philip and Thomas, Bartholomew and Matthew, James son of Alphaeus, Simon the Zealot, and Judas son of James. [14]All these devoted themselves with one accord to prayer, together with some women, and Mary the mother of Jesus, and his brothers.

Notice that this group includes both men and women without distinction. Luke also notes that all are steadfastly devoted to prayer "with one accord" (or "with one mind"), presumably in anticipation of their baptism in the Holy Spirit.

After the story about the selection of Mathias to replace Judas and complete the number of twelve apostles (Acts 1:15-26), Luke continues with the story of the descent of the Holy Spirit upon the early Christian community, giving them the gift of tongues "as the Spirit enabled them to proclaim" (Acts 2:4). Luke does not exclude Mary, the mother of Jesus, and the other women who were part of this early Christian community, so we must assume that they, too, received the Holy Spirit. This first Christian Pentecost took place on the Jewish feast of Pentecost, which takes place fifty days after Passover. Also known as *Shavuot*, or the feast of Weeks, this feast was and is a commemoration of the giving of the law to Moses on Mount Sinai.

Mary, Mother of Jesus, in John's Gospel

The Gospel of John is different in many ways from the Gospels of Matthew, Mark, and Luke, including in the way Mary, the mother of Jesus, is portrayed. The most obvious difference is that, like Mark's Gospel, there is no infancy narrative. However, John's Gospel includes two stories about Mary that are unique to this Gospel. The first is the story of the wedding feast at Cana, and the second is the portrayal of Mary at the crucifixion.

The wedding feast at Cana is the first of seven "signs" narrated in this Gospel. In terms of form, it could otherwise be categorized as a miracle story, but John does not use the term "mighty deed" that the other Gospel writers use to refer to a miracle. Instead, he uses *sémeion*, meaning "sign or token." In the simple sense of the word, let us think about a "sign" as pointing toward something or marking a point along the path to a destination. In John's Gospel, this first sign points to Jesus' glorification, which culminates in his crucifixion and exaltation.

The Cana story appears immediately after John's account of the gathering of Jesus' disciples. Although Mary is the initiator of this first public action in Jesus' ministry, her proper name is never used. Instead, here and throughout John's Gospel, she is always identified as the mother of Jesus (John 2:1, 3, 5, 12; 6:42; 19:25-27).

John 2:1-11

The Wedding at Cana. ¹On the third day there was a wedding in Cana in Galilee, and the mother of Jesus was there. ²Jesus and his disciples were also invited to the wedding. ³When the wine ran short, the mother of Jesus said to him, "They have no wine." ⁴[And] Jesus said to her, "Woman, how does your concern affect me? My hour has not yet come." ⁵His mother said to the servers, "Do whatever he tells you." ⁶Now there were six stone water jars there for Jewish ceremonial washings, each holding twenty to thirty gallons. ⁷Jesus told them, "Fill the jars with water." So they filled them to the brim. ⁸Then he told them, "Draw some out now and take it to the headwaiter." So they took it. ⁹And when the headwaiter tasted the water that had become wine, without knowing where it came from (although the servers who had drawn the water knew), the headwaiter called the bridegroom ¹⁰and said to him, "Everyone serves good wine first, and then when people have drunk freely, an inferior one; but you have kept the good wine until now." ¹¹Jesus did this as the beginning of his signs in Cana in Galilee and so revealed his glory, and his disciples began to believe in him.

The setting of the story is a wedding feast to which Mary and her son Jesus, together with his disciples, have been invited. Wedding ceremonies were public events where the families of the bride and groom declared their alliance with one another for the purpose of protecting family resources and providing male offspring to extend their families' inheritance into the next generation. But in an honor/shame culture, such a public event also held many opportunities for a family to be shamed if the event did not fully conform to cultural expectations, even if this lack of conformity was accidental. Not having enough wine for the feast would have opened the door for a host of criticisms, including that they had put on airs among their peers and then been found out as poorer or less connected socially than everyone thought.

According to the story, Mary is sufficiently connected to these families to be aware of impending disaster, so she goes to her son and says, "They have no wine" (2:3). Notice that she is voicing an observation, not making a request. She is leaving it to Jesus to make a response, but his reply sounds very harsh. The Greek literally reads, "What to me and what to you, woman?" Biblical scholars have gone to great lengths to provide interpretations of this story that do not appear to show Jesus somewhat callously dismissing his mother's concerns. But what if we accept these words as they are? What if John is presenting Jesus as an adult, who, consistent with the culture of the ancient world, is talking down to his mother in a public setting? What if John is signaling that Jesus is about to enter into a new familial relationship—one where he is no longer simply a child of his mother but now the revealer of God in the world (see John 1:18)? This interpretation need not disturb our faith in Jesus' love for Mary. The strength of their relationship is clearly attested by the rest of the Gospel. If anything, it is a helpful reminder that Jesus and Mary were real people who lived in a real place with its own set of cultural norms.

Jesus' response to his mother continues "My hour has not yet come" (2:4). In John's Gospel, Jesus' "hour" is the hour of his death and exaltation, when he has glorified the Father by doing what the Father asked him to do. Are Mary's instructions to the servants ("Do whatever he tells you"; 2:5) an indication that she understands Jesus' "hour" and the salvation story that will unfold in this Gospel? Or does she simply trust that Jesus will do what needs to be done to spare this wedding couple the shame that will befall them when everyone learns that the wine has run out? Perhaps it does not matter what she understands. Her words display the trust she has in Jesus: "Do whatever he tells you." Clearly, Mary believes in Jesus, and in John's Gospel, this makes her a disciple and a child of God (see 1:12-13).

The second and last time that Mary appears in this Gospel is in the crucifixion story (John 19:25-27). Again, John does not use Mary's proper name but instead identifies her simply as Jesus' mother:

John 19:25-27

[25]Standing by the cross of Jesus were his mother and his mother's sister, Mary the wife of Clopas, and Mary of Magdala. [26]When Jesus saw his mother and the disciple there whom he loved, he said to his mother, "Woman, behold, your son." [27]Then he said to the disciple, "Behold, your mother." And from that hour the disciple took her into his home.

Given our knowledge of the culture of the first-century Near East, we might wonder what Mary is thinking and feeling at this moment. Certainly, she must be feeling intense grief. She was present for the beginning of Jesus' ministry, when he changed water to wine at Cana, and now she is present at his death following a conviction of blasphemy and treason. A woman of modest means, now without husband or son, would have been thrust into a difficult and uncertain future. Most likely she would have had to resort to begging to stay alive. Yet John describes her as standing by the cross, a symbol of suffering and death, where she would have been harassed and ridiculed for being where women did not belong. And Jesus, who is in his "hour" and about to enter into the fullness of his glory, gives her a new, more enduring family symbolized by the Beloved Disciple ("the disciple . . . whom he loved"; 19:26).

Just as the author of John's Gospel refers to Mary only as the mother of Jesus, the Beloved Disciple is also not given a proper name. John's Gospel includes other characters who are unnamed, but these two are special. If the Beloved Disciple is the head of the community of believers who identify themselves with this Gospel, then Mary is now fully a part of it. And if Mary is now the mother of the Beloved Disciple, she is also the mother of this community of believers.

 The Woman in Revelation 12 and Our Lady of Guadalupe

Devotion to Mary, the mother of Jesus, is popular among Catholic Christians in different parts of the world, for example, Our Lady of Lourdes in France and Our Lady of Czestochowa in Poland. In the Americas, special devotion is given to Our Lady of Guadalupe because of her two appearances to Juan Diego on Tepeyac Hill (now in Mexico City) in 1531. After Juan Diego carried out the Virgin's instructions, she left her image on the inside of his cloak.

This image has remarkable similarities to the vision of a woman in Revelation 12, who is interpreted by some to be Mary, the mother of Jesus. In 1999, Pope St. John Paul II named Our Lady of Guadalupe as the patroness of the Americas, and he declared Juan Diego a saint in 2002. Her feast day is December 12.

EXPLORING LESSON ONE

1. What is your favorite image of Mary, the mother of Jesus? Why is it attractive to you? Are there any images of Mary that you dislike? Why?

_____

_____

_____

_____

_____

2. Matthew 1:18-25 tells us very little about Mary, the soon-to-be mother of Jesus, and nothing about what she was feeling about her situation. What might Mary have been concerned about when she discovered she was pregnant, especially considering the culture in which she grew up?

_____

_____

_____

_____

_____

3. What message might today's Christian communities draw from the story of the magi who are presented as the first witnesses to the birth of Jesus in Matthew's Gospel (2:1-12)?

_____

_____

_____

_____

4. Luke's story of the conception and birth of Jesus (Luke 1:26-38; 2:1-7) is very different from Matthew's version of the story (Matt 1:18-25), especially in its depiction of Mary. What differences can you identify?

_____

_____

_____

_____

_____

_____

5. How do Luke's infancy narratives alter or expand your view of Mary as a young woman and mother living in first-century Palestine (Luke 1:5–2:52)?

_____

_____

_____

_____

_____

6. Luke's story of Mary's visit to her cousin Elizabeth (Luke 1:39-56), especially the conversation between these two women, can be a powerful and inspiring model for Christians today. How does this story and Mary's song, the *Magnificat*, inspire you in your faith journey?

_____

_____

_____

_____

_____

7. Biblical scholars view Luke's stories of the birth of Jesus (Luke 2:1-7) and the visit by the shepherds (Luke 2:8-20) as illustrations of God's preferential option for the poor, that is, God's special concern for the marginalized in society. What examples can you find in these two texts to support this view?

_____

_____

_____

_____

_____

8. The author of John's Gospel seems to have strategically placed the two stories about the mother of Jesus near the beginning and the end of the Gospel: the wedding feast at Cana (John 2:1-11) and the witness at the crucifixion (John 19:25-27). Can you find any threads that tie these stories together? What message might the author have wanted to convey by positioning these two stories as he did?

_____

_____

_____

_____

_____

9. The Acts of the Apostles describes Mary, the mother of Jesus, as present with the disciples on Pentecost when the Holy Spirit descended on those gathered in the Upper Room (Acts 1:13-14; 2:1-4). For Christians, Pentecost is the birthday of the church and, since the twelfth century, Mary has been known as "Mother of the Church." Given what you know about the portrait of Mary in the Gospels, why is this a fitting title for her? (See also 1 Cor 12:12-13 and Rom 12:3-8.)

_____

_____

_____

_____

_____

CLOSING PRAYER

Prayer

"My soul proclaims the greatness of the Lord;
my spirit rejoices in God my savior."

(Luke 1:46-47)

Gracious and loving God, we thank you for the witness of Mary, the mother of your son, Jesus. She bravely and joyously accepted her role in service of humanity's salvation by allowing herself to be labeled as an unmarried pregnant woman and later to witness the shameful death of her son. May we be inspired by her courage and dedication as we honor her as Mother of the Church today. Inspired by Mary's example, we pray today especially for . . .

LESSON TWO

Women Beneficiaries of Jesus' Miracles

Begin your personal study and group discussion with a simple and sincere prayer such as:

Prayer

God of love and consolation, as we study the women of the New Testament, open our hearts and minds to appreciate the unique gifts they each brought to their faith communities. May their witness inspire us today to use the gifts we have received in service of your holy ones.

Read pages 32–41, Lesson Two, highlighting what stands out to you.

Respond to the questions on pages 42–45, Exploring Lesson Two.

The Closing Prayer on page 45 is for your personal use and may be used at the end of group discussion.

WOMEN BENEFICIARIES OF JESUS' MIRACLES

The New Testament Gospels contain a large number of miracle stories—thirty-seven, by some people's count—including several stories featuring women as the recipients of Jesus' mighty deeds. In this lesson, we will examine several of these stories to see what they reveal about the lives of women who lived on the margins of society because of illness or misfortune.

Given modern skepticism about miracles, it might be helpful to summarize what we know about miracle-working in the first-century Eastern Mediterranean world. In their book *Social-Science Commentary on the Synoptic Gospels*, Bruce Malina and Richard Rohrbaugh note that anthropologists distinguish between *disease* and *illness*. *Disease* has to do with the biomedical malfunction of an organism such as the human body. *Illness*, however, involves a deviation from cultural values and expectations, even though there might be an underlying physical condition that prompts the illness and the need for healing. Further, they note that Jesus' healing miracles generally involve *illnesses*—that is, a disvaluing of the human person resulting from disruptions to social networks. Finally, they give the example of leprosy, which is known today as Hansen's disease, a treatable medical condition caused by slow-growing bacteria. We know how to treat the *disease* today, but in the New Testament world, it was considered an *illness* that isolated an individual and disrupted social networks like families and working relationships.

John Pilch, a biblical scholar who specializes in medical anthropology, takes this distinction between disease and illness a step further in his book *Healing in the New Testament*. He describes *health* as a particular culture's comprehensive understanding of physical, mental, and social

Medical Terminology	Definition
Disease	As understood in the modern Western world, the biomedical malfunction of an organism.
Curing	As understood in the modern Western world, the ability to manage or take control of biological or psychological symptoms.
Illness	In the first-century Near Eastern world, a deviation from cultural values and expectations, which may or may not have been brought about by an underlying physical condition, but which resulted in isolation and fractured relationships.
Healing	In the first-century Near Eastern world, making life meaningful and providing support within the community for those who are ill, regardless of whether their physical symptoms were alleviated.

well-being, not simply as the absence of disease. Further, he associates disease with *curing*, the ability to manage or take control of biological or psychological symptoms. By contrast, *healing*, which anthropologists associate with illness (as defined above), is concerned with providing meaning and support for those who are ill.

A modern comparison might help to explain. Someone who is suffering through multiple courses of chemotherapy to cure rapidly advancing cancer might become so sick and discouraged that he or she feels like life has little meaning. Our modern medical system is amazing, but one of its challenges is keeping the person, not the disease, at the center of attention. We are gradually learning the importance of a strong and supportive social network of family, friends, and caregivers as an essential part of making life meaningful and worth living for the one who is sick, regardless of whether the disease is cured. From a biblical perspective, this is what healing is all about.

In summary, modern skepticism about miracles is rooted in the disease/cure model, while ancients were more focused on the illness/healing model. This does not discount the possibility of miraculous cures today or in the ancient world. Indeed, some of the Gospel stories we will examine together describe the curing of physical ailments. But the point here is that in order to fully appreciate the miracle stories of the Gospels, it is important to understand them in their cultural context, one that valued healing over curing. Disease and other maladies were everywhere in the ancient world, and average life expectancy is estimated to have been around forty-five years. Whether or not someone was *cured of their disease*, they could be *healed of the illness* of isolation and fractured relations. Ancient Eastern Mediterranean cultures did not have anything like our modern medical system, but they knew well the power of community for improving a person's well-being and giving meaning to life.

 In ancient Israel and early Judaism (sixth century BCE–70 CE), God's people recognized physical phenomena like wind, rain, and movement of the sun, moon, and stars as **miracles**, that is, physical manifestations of a personal God's love and care for creation. The psalms speak to this belief in clear and convincing ways (e.g., Ps 72 and 136). Reflect on the ways your life story is a series of miracles given to you as manifestations of a personal God's love for you.

Equally important to the interpretation of miracle stories is understanding their literary form or structural pattern. Biblical scholars have observed at least three key structural elements in any miracle story: (1) a description of the problem, (2) the miracle worker's word or action that effects the miracle, and (3) evidence that the miracle took place. These elements are usually easy to find, but when the Gospel writer alters these elements in some way, we must pay special attention. For example, if Jesus is described as healing someone in private and asking the person who is healed not to tell anyone, but the sick person does anyway, we should consider the significance of this detail and its meaning for the larger message of the Gospel. Sometimes the Gospel writer adds dialogue or another story within or surrounding the miracle story. Any of these additional elements are useful for discerning the meaning of the miracle story and the Gospel as a whole.

We might also ask what it means that Jesus was able to work miracles. Some theologians have argued that Jesus' ability to perform miracles is proof that he was divine, but then we are faced with the problem of biblical accounts of other miracle workers in both testaments of the Bible, including Jesus' own disciples (e.g., Matt 10:1; Mark 3:15; Luke 9:1-2). Are they all divine?

In his article "Jesus as Healer" (published by the Center for Christian Ethics at Baylor University), John Pilch reminds readers that Scripture tells us medical professionals are important, but God is the one who heals (see Sir 38:1-15). He also notes that although New Testament translations use the terms "doctor" and "physician," these medical professionals were more like philosophers than the doctors or physicians we know today. By contrast, Jesus would have been viewed as a folk healer in his culture and as a powerful intercessor with God in the eyes of the community of believers. It takes an exceedingly holy person to effect so many miracles on behalf of God. This is Jesus, the healer, who gives meaning to the lives of those who suffer the alienating effects of illness.

With this sociocultural and literary background in mind, let us examine some of the Gospel stories about women who encounter Jesus the healer. We will begin with Mark's stories of the healing of the hemorrhaging woman and the raising of Jairus's daughter (Mark 5:21-43; see also Matt 9:18-26; Luke 8:40-56). Next, we will look at the story of the healing of a Syrophoenician woman's daughter (Mark 7:24-30; Matt 15:21-28) and, after that, four more stories that involve female characters who encounter Jesus in their quest for healing.

The Gospels of Matthew, Mark, and Luke are called **Synoptic Gospels** because they "read the same" or come from the same point of view. Biblical scholars are still debating the relationship among these three Gospels, but most accept the Two Source Hypothesis, which posits that Mark wrote his Gospel first, and that Matthew and Luke then used Mark and a collection of sayings of Jesus (which scholars have named "Q"), along with some additional materials known to their own communities in order to write their Gospels.

Healing of the Hemorrhaging Woman and Raising of Jairus's Daughter

The stories of the healing of the hemorrhaging woman and the raising of Jairus's daughter have an interesting literary structure called *intercalation*, in which one story is inserted within another. At first glance, intercalated stories might seem unrelated, but there is usually a literary connection between the two stories. More importantly, the inner story usually gives us clues about how the outer story might be interpreted.

Let us first analyze the inner story, the healing of a hemorrhaging woman, as it appears in Mark's Gospel:

Mark 5:25-34

[25]There was a woman afflicted with hemorrhages for twelve years. [26]She had suffered greatly at the hands of many doctors and had spent all that she had. Yet she was not helped but only grew worse. [27]She had heard about Jesus and came up behind him in the crowd and touched his cloak. [28]She said, "If I but touch his clothes, I shall be cured." [29]Immediately her flow of blood dried up. She felt in her body that she was healed of her affliction. [30]Jesus, aware at once that power had gone out from him, turned around in the crowd and asked, "Who has touched my clothes?" [31]But his disciples said to him, "You see how the crowd is pressing upon you, and yet you ask, 'Who touched me?'" [32]And he looked around to see who had done it. [33]The woman, realizing what had happened to her, approached in fear and trembling. She fell down before Jesus and told him the whole truth. [34]He said to her, "Daughter, your faith has saved you. Go in peace and be cured of your affliction."

In terms of form, the first element of this miracle story—the description of the problem—is filled with detail and great angst. Although the translation from the New American Bible,

Revised Edition (NABRE) is punctuated for easier reading, in Greek, 5:25-27 comprise a single sentence containing many gerunds (verbs that function as nouns and end in -*ing*). This is how a more literal translation might read:

> And a woman, being with a flowing of blood for twelve years and having suffered much under many physicians and having spent all of what she had and having benefitted in no way but rather having gotten worse, having heard about Jesus, and having come up behind him in the crowd, touched his clothing.

As you can see, even the sentence structure shouts anxiety! It is nearly impossible to read this three-verse sentence in a single breath. And when you have fully grasped the content of these three verses both mentally and emotionally, all you can say is "This poor woman!"

Mark's narrative provides us with several important clues about the woman's situation. First, there is no mention of an adult male in her life: no husband, no son, no father, no brother. She is most likely alone in life because her constant hemorrhaging makes her perpetually ritually unclean, a condition that excludes her from the regular life of the community. Her hemorrhage is described as a "fountain of blood" and as a "scourge" or "plague" (5:29, my translation). We are told that the woman has had this condition for twelve years, during which time she would have been incapable of bearing children. The number twelve is a symbol of fullness or completeness. Thus, the length of her illness means that she could not be an effective wife and mother for the full length of her adulthood. The narrator also tells us that she has suffered much and spent all she had on many physicians. Remember that these were medical professionals or philosophers of medicine. Only the wealthy could afford these physicians, and now she is too poor to seek other cures from them. Can you sense her desperation?

The second and third elements of a miracle story are the miracle worker's word or deed that effects the miracle, and evidence that the miracle has taken place. The narrator of this story covers the third element by saying that the woman "felt in her body" that her hemorrhage was healed and that Jesus felt energy go out of his body when she touched him (5:29-30). But what about the second element of the story? The woman does not approach Jesus directly to make a request for healing. Instead, she slips through the crowd that is pressing in on Jesus and touches his outer garment, thinking that would be enough for her healing. Notice her reaction when Jesus asks, "Who has touched my clothes?" (5:30). We are told that she approaches Jesus "in fear and trembling" (5:33). Does she fear that she will be "outed" as someone who must be excluded from the community? Not so! Jesus calls her "Daughter" (5:34), establishing her as a member of God's family. But Jesus himself does nothing to heal her. Rather, he simply says, "[Y]our faith has saved you" (5:34). Note that the perfect form of the Greek verb *sózó*, which is used here, means "has made whole" or "has rescued." Amazing! This woman, whose first reaction to her healing is described in terms of fear and shame, is the one who effected the miracle on God's behalf because of her faith.

Now let us analyze the outer story of this intercalation.

Mark 5:21-43

Jairus's Daughter and the Woman with a Hemorrhage. [21]When Jesus had crossed again [in the boat] to the other side, a large crowd gathered around him, and he stayed close to the sea. [22]One of the synagogue officials, named Jairus, came forward. Seeing him he fell at his feet [23]and pleaded earnestly with him, saying, "My daughter is at the point of death. Please, come lay your hands on her that she may get well and live." [24]He went off with him, and a large crowd followed him and pressed upon him.

[The story of the hemorrhaging woman (5:25-34) fits here.]

continue

³⁵While he was still speaking, people from the synagogue official's house arrived and said, "Your daughter has died; why trouble the teacher any longer?" ³⁶Disregarding the message that was reported, Jesus said to the synagogue official, "Do not be afraid; just have faith." ³⁷He did not allow anyone to accompany him inside except Peter, James, and John, the brother of James. ³⁸When they arrived at the house of the synagogue official, he caught sight of a commotion, people weeping and wailing loudly. ³⁹So he went in and said to them, "Why this commotion and weeping? The child is not dead but asleep." ⁴⁰And they ridiculed him. Then he put them all out. He took along the child's father and mother and those who were with him and entered the room where the child was. ⁴¹He took the child by the hand and said to her, "*Talitha koum*," which means, "Little girl, I say to you, arise!" ⁴²The girl, a child of twelve, arose immediately and walked around. [At that] they were utterly astounded. ⁴³He gave strict orders that no one should know this and said that she should be given something to eat.

As the story begins, we might imagine that this outer story will be a healing miracle similar to the inner story. However, by the time we reach the second half of the story, we discover that this is actually a resuscitation, a bringing back to life. We are told that Jairus is a high-ranking synagogue official, perhaps its patron. When he begs and bows down before Jesus, a simple folk healer, he dishonors himself in this very public setting (5:22-23). Such is Jairus's level of desperation!

When Jairus requests assistance for his child, he calls her his "little daughter" (5:23, my translation). The narrator then says, "He went off with him" (5:24). Did Jesus go off with Jairus, or did Jairus follow Jesus? The Greek text does not indicate which is which, but the latter would be perceived as a further diminishment of Jairus's honor. Notice also that Jesus has not yet voiced a response to Jairus's request for his daughter's healing. Poor Jairus is made to follow Jesus into the scene of the healing

of the hemorrhaging woman without any acknowledgment by Jesus that his situation will be remedied.

After Jesus leaves the scene of the healing of the hemorrhaging woman, we learn that Jairus's daughter has already died. His servants bring this news to Jairus and tell him there is no need to bother Jesus any further. Although Jairus does not respond to his servants, Jesus reassures him, "Do not be afraid; just have faith" (5:36). When they arrive at Jairus's home, they witness all kinds of commotion because the funeral arrangements are already underway. Although our knowledge of first-century Jewish burials is limited, we can imagine that the girl's body is already being washed, wrapped in a shroud, and prepared for the procession to the burial place. Burials had to take place quickly to preserve the dignity of the dead.

When Jesus tells those who are gathered that the child is not dead but asleep, the narrator tells us that they "ridiculed" him (5:40). The Greek word *katagelaó*, meaning "to deride" or "to laugh, to scorn," is used in the New Testament only here and in this story's parallels in Matthew 9:18-26 and Luke 8:40-56. Why were these people so hostile and insulting toward Jesus? While they might have accepted Jesus' status as a folk healer, they knew the child was dead, and they also believed that no one except God could raise the dead. "This Jesus is making crazy talk," we might imagine them saying!

The narrator then tells us that Jesus makes those who ridiculed him leave the premises. He enters the room where the child is lying. He takes the girl's hand and calls to her, "Little girl, I say to you, arise!" (5:41). This is the second element of a miracle story, the miracle worker's healing word or deed. This is also when we learn that the girl is twelve years of age. Without Jesus' intervention, she would have been deprived of her womanhood, much like the woman who was hemorrhaging for twelve years. The third element, evidence that the miracle has taken place, is found in the narrator's comment that the girl "arose immediately and walked around" (5:42) and in Jesus' command that the parents give the girl something to eat (5:43). After all, ghosts cannot eat food!

Perhaps you have already noticed some of the literary connections between these intercalated stories. As noted above, the number twelve and the word "daughter" are used in both stories. Both stories depict someone falling down or prostrating themselves before Jesus, and a group of people who express incredulity over something Jesus says. In the inner story, it is Jesus' disciples; in the outer story, it is the people who are trying to bury the girl. Likewise, there is a reference to fear in both stories. In the story of the resuscitation of Jairus's daughter, Jesus tells Jairus, "Do not be afraid; just have faith" (5:36). But, as noted earlier, the inner story often carries the central message of the intercalation. Here is this woman who has been deprived of life on so many levels. However, despite her fear, she reaches out to Jesus, who calls her "daughter" and declares that her faith made her well (5:34). The message to Jairus and to all of us is that faith, understood as trust in the God who lives,

can work miracles by restoring us to fullness of life in community.

Healing of the Syrophoenician Woman's Daughter

Another story from Mark's Gospel that showcases a woman who encounters Jesus the healer is the story of a foreign woman who seeks healing for her daughter who is possessed by a demon (Mark 7:24-30; see also Matt 15:21-28). The opening sentence of this story indicates that Jesus' fame was spreading even to non-Jewish territories such as Tyre, an important trade city in the region of Phoenicia, which was located north and west of Galilee. Tyre was especially known for its production of linen, purple dye, and a fermented fish sauce called *garum*. We are not told why Jesus sought to enter this house without anyone noticing, but we might think of it as an ancient equivalent of today's celebrities trying to avoid the paparazzi. He needed some privacy!

This image of a woman requesting healing for her daughter is based on Matthew 15:21-28 rather than Mark 7:24-30. Can you tell why? Hint: Note the setting of the story in both accounts.

Mark 7:24-30

The Syrophoenician Woman's Faith. ²⁴From that place he went off to the district of Tyre. He entered a house and wanted no one to know about it, but he could not escape notice. ²⁵Soon a woman whose daughter had an unclean spirit heard about him. She came and fell at his feet. ²⁶The woman was a Greek, a Syrophoenician by birth, and she begged him to drive the demon out of her daughter. ²⁷He said to her, "Let the children be fed first. For it is not right to take the food of the children and throw it to the dogs." ²⁸She replied and said to him, "Lord, even the dogs under the table eat the children's scraps." ²⁹Then he said to her, "For saying this, you may go. The demon has gone out of your daughter." ³⁰When the woman went home, she found the child lying in bed and the demon gone.

We do not know the name of this woman who seeks Jesus out. Who is she, and how does she know where to find Jesus? How does she, a Gentile woman from a predominantly Gentile territory, know Jesus is a healer? After all, she would be considered an outsider to Jesus' circle of disciples. What right does she have to approach Jesus for a healing? The irony, of course, is that Jesus is the one who is an outsider in Tyre.

First-century Jews and early Christians were not the only ones who believed in a healing deity. Perhaps the most widely known source of healings in the Greco-Roman world was the **Asclepius cult**. Asclepius was trained in the healing arts and, upon his death, he was raised to the status of a god. Temples to Asclepius had places for purification rituals, dream therapy, restful sleep, dining, and visits with healers.

Jesus' response, very much in keeping with his time and place, is not a pleasant one. He answers her with a riddle: "Let the children be fed first. For it is not right to take the food of the children and throw it to the dogs" (7:27). The "food" represents God's life-saving miracles. The "children" are God's chosen people, the Jews. And here is where things get very nasty. Jesus rather pointedly suggests that the woman and the people she represents are "dogs"— little, ritually unclean scavengers. Not to be deterred, and despite the assault on her honor, the woman responds respectfully but forthrightly: "Lord, even the dogs under the table eat the children's scraps" (7:28). Surprisingly, these words effect her daughter's exorcism (7:29). Was she aware of the power of her words?

Biblical scholars have debated over the interpretation of this story. Is Jesus testing her to see if she has enough faith (i.e., trust in God) to make an exception on her behalf and use his

Asclepius with serpent-enwrapped staff. Note the similarities with the modern symbol for the medical profession.

agency to heal this Gentile woman's daughter? Alternatively, is this story being used to show how Jesus came to understand that God's healing power should not be restricted to the Jews alone but is available to all humanity? In support of the former, someone might note that Mark presents Jesus as performing an exorcism in Gentile territory earlier in the Gospel (see Mark 5:1-20). In support of the latter, the statement ascribed to Jesus in this story is significant: "*Because of this word*, go; the demon has gone forth out of your daughter" (7:29, my translation). If this is what Mark intended, perhaps this woman is teaching Jesus about his own ministry. What do you think?

Healing of Peter's Mother-in-Law

Mark's Gospel provides one more very brief story about the healing of a woman, namely the story of Jesus healing Peter's mother-in-law (Mark 1:29-31; see also Matt 8:14-15; Luke 4:38-39). Because this story is so short, one might think it is not important, but it contains all three of the basic elements of a miracle story and little more, leaving some biblical scholars to suggest that it is a direct transfer of an oral tradition from the time of Jesus to the written text composed some forty years later.

Mark 1:29-31

The Cure of Simon's Mother-in-Law. [29]On leaving the synagogue he entered the house of Simon and Andrew with James and John. [30]Simon's mother-in-law lay sick with a fever. They immediately told him about her. [31]He approached, grasped her hand, and helped her up. Then the fever left her and she waited on them.

A few things are of note here. First, like the other stories about women's healings described above, this woman has no name. Second, we can assume that Peter's mother-in-law lived with Peter and his wife and whatever children they might have had. Such was the practice of the time. Third, although as contemporary readers we might be troubled by the apparent sexism of this story—"Then the fever left her and she waited on them" (1:31)—it is Mark's way of verifying that this healing took place; her relationships and her active role within her family have been restored. Some biblical scholars have also noted that the Greek verb *diakoneó*, translated here as "to wait upon," also means "to minister to." You can hear our English word "deacon" in the pronunciation of this word. Is Mark suggesting that this woman was a forerunner of the female deacons of a decade or two later (see Lesson Six)?

Raising of a Widow's Son and Healing of a Woman Who Is "Bent Over"

Biblical scholars have long noted that Luke's Gospel contains many more stories about women than any other Gospel of the New Testament. This realization has led some people to conclude that Luke intended to elevate the status of women above their prescribed place in first-century Jewish or Gentile societies. However, a close look at Luke's stories about women indicates that, despite the prominence of women in his Gospel, Luke was very much a product of his time.

Two stories that are found only in Luke's Gospel illustrate this point. The first is the story of the raising of a widow's son. Biblical scholars have observed that Luke tends to pair a story that has a man as one of its major characters with a story that has a woman as a major character. Just prior to this scene, Jesus is described as healing a Roman centurion's male slave in the city of Capernaum (Luke 7:1-10).

Luke's story of the raising of the deceased son of the widow of Nain depicts a woman whose tether to community relationships is extremely fragile:

Luke 7:11-17

Raising of the Widow's Son. [11]Soon afterward he journeyed to a city called Nain, and his disciples and a large crowd accompanied him. [12]As he drew near to the gate of the city, a man who had died was being carried out, the only son of his mother, and she was a widow. A large crowd from the city was with her. [13]When the Lord saw her, he was moved with pity for her and said to her, "Do not weep." [14]He stepped forward and touched the coffin; at this the bearers halted, and he said, "Young man, I tell you, arise!" [15]The dead man sat up and began to speak, and Jesus gave him to his mother. [16]Fear seized them all, and they glorified God, exclaiming, "A great prophet has arisen in our midst," and "God has visited his people." [17]This report about him spread through the whole of Judea and in all the surrounding region.

A first-century Mediterranean woman's identity was primarily defined by her marital and maternal status, a status that was enhanced if she was the mother of male children. Luke quickly describes the woman in this story as a widow who is burying her only son. Her grief must have been tinged with terror about how she would survive her losses. A widowed woman with no sons and without wealth of her own would be forced to beg (or worse) to stay alive.

But this widow does not approach Jesus for a remedy to her situation. Why would she? Her son is dead, and only God can raise the dead. When Jesus approaches her, having been moved with compassion at the sight of her, he tells her not to mourn or lament. Note that Luke does not give the woman a voice, but when Jesus addresses the corpse with the word "arise!" (7:14), the young man sits up and begins to speak, thereby restoring the woman's motherhood.

The woman and her son have both been healed. What must she be thinking after such an experience? How might Jesus' compassion have impacted her view on life?

The second of these stories found only in Luke's Gospel is the story of the healing of a woman who is "crippled" or "bent over":

Luke 13:10-17

Cure of a Crippled Woman on the Sabbath. [10]He was teaching in a synagogue on the sabbath. [11]And a woman was there who for eighteen years had been crippled by a spirit; she was bent over, completely incapable of standing erect. [12]When Jesus saw her, he called to her and said, "Woman, you are set free of your infirmity." [13]He laid his hands on her, and she at once stood up straight and glorified God. [14]But the leader of the synagogue, indignant that Jesus had cured on the sabbath, said to the crowd in reply, "There are six days when work should be done. Come on those days to be cured, not on the sabbath day." [15]The Lord said to him in reply, "Hypocrites! Does not each one of you on the sabbath untie his ox or his ass from the manger and lead it out for watering? [16]This daughter of Abraham, whom Satan has bound for eighteen years now, ought she not to have been set free on the sabbath day from this bondage?" [17]When he said this, all his adversaries were humiliated; and the whole crowd rejoiced at all the splendid deeds done by him.

Unlike in most miracle stories, where the supplicant initiates contact with the miracle worker, Jesus is the one to notice this "bent" woman, who is already present in the synagogue. Can we assume that she is a devout Jew? The narrator tells us that she has suffered this infirmity for eighteen years, likely at least half of her life. The Greek word *sugkuptó* means "bent" or "crooked." The disease was probably ankylosing spondylitis (*spondylitis ankylopoietica*), an inflammatory disease that affects the spine and pelvic joints and can even result in fusion of the spinal column, resulting in lung and heart problems. This disease begins to manifest itself in early adulthood, is not curable, and creates the greatest damage to the spine in the first ten years of its progression.

Luke's "bent" woman probably is not able to raise her eyes high enough to see Jesus. Most likely, she can only see a small space around her feet, and her walking is most certainly unsteady. Did anyone think to provide her with a cane, at least? Jesus calls to her, but the narrator does not give her a voice to respond. Now Jesus comes close enough to lay hands on her—Can she see his feet?—and the narrator says, "Immediately she *was straightened out* and she kept on praising God" (13:13, my translation). Biblical scholars call this use of the passive voice the *divine passive*, meaning that God, who is unnamed, effects the miracle. Jesus is the agent of God's activity in the world.

The rest of the story involves a conflict between Jesus and the leader of the synagogue over what work can be performed on the Sabbath. The synagogue leader says that the healing of this woman, who has suffered under the burden of her illness for eighteen years, can wait one more day. Luke portrays Jesus as doing two things: calling the woman a "daughter of Abraham" (13:16), thus restoring and asserting her community relationship, and comparing her situation to that of a farm animal on the Sabbath. If Jewish law allows for care of an animal—a beast of burden—on the Sabbath, doesn't she deserve the same? But here is an added paradox. The woman has withdrawn into the background of the story, despite the fact that she is the central figure in this conflict between Jesus and the leader of the synagogue.

As we conclude this lesson, you are invited to consider your own life story. Whether young or old, male or female, there will be times in all of our lives when we need healing and restoration to whole and healthy relationships, both within ourselves and among others. Hopefully one or another of these healing stories will inspire you to seek healing and to be the agent of healing for others in Jesus' name.

EXPLORING LESSON TWO

1. What is your view of miracles? Have you witnessed or experienced a miracle? Describe in your own words the difference between curing a disease (a typical modern Western view) and healing an illness (the ancient Mediterranean view).

_____

_____

_____

_____

_____

_____

_____

_____

2. a) Carefully examine Mark's intercalated stories of the healing of the woman with the hemorrhage and the raising of Jairus's daughter (Mark 5:21-43). Locate the three basic elements of a miracle story in each of these stories. Can you see where the pattern is altered in the inner story? What is unique about the healing of the hemorrhaging woman?

_____

_____

_____

_____

_____

_____

   b) Find the words or phrases that link these two stories together. If the inner story helps to inform or explain the outer story, what seems to be the message that Mark wants to convey with these intercalated stories?

_____

_____

_____

_____

_____

_____

_____

3. Read Matthew's version of these intercalated stories, which was likely written a decade after Mark's, using Mark's version as a source (Matt 9:18-26). Do you find it more or less interesting than Mark's version (Mark 5:21-43)? In what way? What are the benefits of comparing different versions of the same Gospel story?

_____

_____

_____

_____

_____

_____

_____

4. Mark's story of the healing of the Syrophoenician woman's daughter (Mark 7:24-30) can be interpreted in two very different ways, and the Gospel text does not tell us which interpretation Mark intended. Which interpretation do you prefer? Why?

_____

_____

_____

_____

_____

_____

_____

5. Compare Matthew's version of the healing of the foreign woman's daughter (Matt 15:21-28) to Mark's version of the same story (Mark 7:24-30). Assuming that Mark's Gospel was written first, make a list of the details Matthew retained from Mark's story. Make another list of details Matthew changed. Why might Matthew have made these choices? What effect do they have on how the story is read or interpreted?

_____

_____

_____

_____

_____

_____

_____

_____

6. Mark's story of the healing of Peter's mother-in-law is very short, but it has the three basic elements of a miracle story (Mark 1:29-31). See if you can identify them. Stories written such a long time ago do not necessarily address questions modern readers may have when reading the story. What question would you like to ask the author of this story?

_____

_____

_____

_____

_____

_____

_____

7. Luke's story of the raising of the son of the widow of Nain ends with the narrator saying that "fear seized them all" (Luke 7:11-17). The word "fear" might be better translated as "amazement" or "awe." If you were part of the funeral procession, what would have caused you to be amazed? What words or images come to mind when you hear the phrase "God has visited his people"?

_____

_____

_____

_____

_____

_____

8. Luke's story of the healing of the woman who is "bent over" (Luke 13:11-17) can be extremely evocative for anyone who has witnessed a loved one struggling with severe scoliosis in their later years. While Luke does not give this woman a voice, you can. Use your imagination to place yourself in the story. Give this woman a name and provide her with words to speak to Jesus and/or the leader of the synagogue. In what ways can you identify with this woman in your own life?

_____

_____

_____

_____

_____

_____

_____

9. If we think of healing miracles as *healing an illness* rather than *curing a disease*—much like first-century Mediterranean peoples did—then perhaps we can play at least some small part in effecting healing in those around us. Select one of the miracle stories in this lesson and prayerfully reflect on it. Does the woman in the story remind you of anyone, male or female, among your family or friends? What is the healing that person most needs in order to find meaning and support in his or her time of illness? What can you do to aid in that healing?

CLOSING PRAYER

Prayer

"Lord, even the dogs under the table eat the children's scraps." (Mark 7:28)

Good and gracious God, we thank you for the Gospel stories of the many unnamed women who sought healing and restoration to community life through the mighty deeds of your son Jesus. In particular, we thank you for the woman who was audacious enough to counter Jesus when he said, "Let the children be fed first" (Mark 7:27), in order to save her daughter. May the stories of all these women inspire us to be bold in our faith and to steadfastly pursue encounters with the One who can set us free and bring new life. Inspired by their example, we pray today especially for . . .

LESSON THREE

The Samaritan Woman of John's Gospel

Begin your personal study and group discussion with a simple and sincere prayer such as:

Prayer

God of love and consolation, as we study the women of the New Testament, open our hearts and minds to appreciate the unique gifts they each brought to their faith communities. May their witness inspire us today to use the gifts we have received in service of your holy ones.

Read pages 48–57, Lesson Three, highlighting what stands out to you.

Respond to the questions on pages 58–60, Exploring Lesson Three.

The Closing Prayer on page 61 is for your personal use and may be used at the end of group discussion.

THE SAMARITAN WOMAN
OF JOHN'S GOSPEL

The Gospel of John contains several stories about women that are different from those of the Synoptic Gospels. We have already looked at John's portrayal of Mary, the mother of Jesus, at the wedding feast in Cana and at the crucifixion. But this Gospel also highlights some women who appear nowhere else in the New Testament. John's rather detailed and somewhat symbolic story of the Samaritan woman's encounter with Jesus (John 4:4-42) is a perfect example.

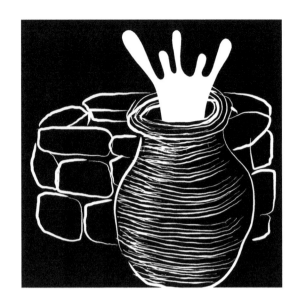

Who Are the Samaritans?

There are at least two things we need to know before delving deeply into this story. First, we need to know who the Samaritans were (and are) and what their relationship with the Judeans (here called Jews) to the south was like in first-century Palestine. The origin of the Samaritan people dates back to the Assyrian conquest of the northern kingdom of Israel in 722 BCE. To maintain their vast empire, the Assyrians practiced deportation of conquered peoples and settlement of their own people in their place. Those Israelites in the northern kingdom who were not deported came to be known as Samaritans. Later, the southern kingdom of Judea came under assault by the Babylonians (c. 597 BCE), the Jerusalem temple was destroyed, and the elite of the southern kingdom were exiled to Babylon.

When the Judeans were allowed to return to Jerusalem and begin to rebuild the temple some seventy years later (see Jer 29:10), the Samaritans opposed them. This opposition, along with other negative encounters over time (exacerbated by both sides), created significant animosities between these two peoples. Here are just a few literary examples of the virulence of the partisanship between Samaritans and Jews that endures in some form even today:

- "My whole being loathes two nations, / the third is not even a people: / The inhabitants of Seir and Philistia, / and the foolish people who dwell in Shechem" (Sir 50:25-26). Shechem was the center of Samaritan worship at the time Sirach was written (c. 180 BCE).

- "R. Eliezer said, 'He that eats the bread of the Samaritans is like one who eats the flesh of swine'" (*Mishnah Shevi'it* 8:10). The Mishnah, a collection of oral traditions from the third century CE, is attributed to the rabbis of early Judaism, but many of the sayings are thought to have originated in the first century CE. Observant Jews do not eat pork or any of its byproducts at any time (see Deut 14:8-10).

- "The daughters of Samaria are deemed unclean as menstruants from their cradle" (*Mishnah Niddah* 4:1). *Mishnah Niddah* belongs to a section of the Mishnah that deals with Jewish purity regulations concerning menstruating women, or women in the birthing process. To say that a Samaritan girl or woman is *never* ritually pure is an especially harsh judgment.

Although once numbering more than a million adherents, there are now approximately eight hundred Samaritans living in Holon, near Tel Aviv in Israel, and in Kiryat Luza on Mount Gerizim, near Nablus and the ancient city of Shechem on the West Bank. Samaritans accept only their Pentateuch, which they believe predates the Pentateuch of the Jews. Their primary center of worship is Mount Gerizim, and their religious rituals appear to be older than those of Second Temple Judaism (c. 515 BCE–70 CE). Claiming to be descendants of the tribes of Ephraim, Manasseh, and Levi, they see themselves as the true Israelites and keepers of the covenant that God made with Moses.

 The term **"Second Temple Judaism"** refers to the developments in early Judaism that took place between the time of the rebuilding of the Jerusalem temple in approximately 538–515 BCE (after the Babylonian Exile) and the destruction of the Jerusalem temple by the Romans in 70 CE. During this period, hostilities between Samaritans and Jews grew significantly, especially after John Hyrcanus, high priest of the Jerusalem temple, destroyed the Samaritans' temple on Mount Gerazim in 112–111 BCE.

Literary Forms and Techniques Used in John's Gospel

Before we launch into an investigation of the story of the Samaritan woman, it will also be helpful for us to understand some of the literary features of the Gospel of John. Otherwise, we are apt to miss the deeper layers of meaning that the Gospel writer wants to impart to his readers.

One important but often overlooked literary feature of any narration is the role of the narrator, who has deep insight into what is happening in the story. In John's Gospel, the narrator is not an outsider looking in on the scene but rather an insider who is even able to read the minds of characters and tell us what they are feeling. Further, the narrator draws the reader into the story so effectively that we can imagine ourselves standing shoulder to shoulder with the narrator and seeing and hearing exactly what he sees and hears. Sometimes it is as if the narrator turns his head toward us and whispers in our ear some bit of information that we need to know in order to better understand the story. Biblical scholars call this technique an *explanatory note*. An example from the story of the Samaritan woman is the statement "For Jews use nothing in common with Samaritans" (John 4:9). The narrator is signaling to the reader that Jesus' request for water is a potentially problematic act.

Another technique used by the author of John's Gospel is *dualism*, the juxtaposition of opposite elements like light and darkness, truth and falsehood, and "from above" and "from below." Whenever you see these polar opposites, you can think in terms of acceptance of Jesus, who is the revealer of God. Those who walk in the light, know the truth, and are born "from above" have placed their trust in Jesus. Those who stumble in the dark, speak falsehoods, and are "from below" have rejected Jesus or have not yet allied themselves with him. In the story of the Samaritan woman, for example, we learn that she encounters Jesus at noon, the brightest time of the day. However, in the story that precedes this one, Nicodemus comes to Jesus at night (3:2). Although he appears to say all the right words when he first meets Jesus, at the end all he can say is "How can this happen?" (3:9). Thus, Nicodemus continues to walk in darkness. By contrast, after her encounter with Jesus, the Samaritan woman professes her faith in him to the whole town (4:29). Clearly, she walks in the light!

Yet another common feature of this Gospel is the use of *irony*, where characters in the story say or do something that is intended to be sarcastic, derogatory, or otherwise belittling while the reader properly understands the deeper truth or meaning of the statement or scene. For example, in the trial of Jesus before Pontius Pilate as told in John's Gospel, the Roman soldiers mockingly dress the bruised and bloody Jesus in a purple robe, place a crown of thorns on his head, and address him, saying, "Hail, King of the Jews" (19:2-3). The irony for the believer is that Jesus truly *is* the king of the Jews. In the story of the Samaritan woman, Jesus tells the woman that if she knew who she was speaking to, she would have asked him for "living water" (4:10). She responds by saying, "You are not greater than our father Jacob who gave us this well and drank from it himself and his sons and his livestock, are you?" (4:12, my translation). Can you sense the disdain and sarcasm in her words? But the believer who hears this story knows that Jesus truly is greater than Jacob.

John's Gospel also presents Jesus as using words that have double meanings. The characters in conversation with Jesus often misunderstand him because they assume the plain meaning of the word. But their misunderstanding allows Jesus to expound on the deeper meaning of the word, offering clarification to characters in the story as well as readers of the Gospel. For example, in the Nicodemus story that precedes the story of the Samaritan woman, Jesus says to Nicodemus, "Unless one is born *anóthen*, they cannot see the kingdom of God" (3:3, my translation). Nicodemus understands only one meaning of *anóthen*—"again"—and so he thinks Jesus is saying that he must crawl back in his mother's womb and be born again (3:4). But *anóthen* can also mean "from above." Thus, Jesus expands on his teaching by saying, "If one is not born of water and the Spirit, they cannot enter the kingdom of God" (3:5, my translation). We will see several more of these double meanings and misunderstandings in the story of the Samaritan woman.

Finally, the author of John's Gospel structures some of the Gospel's more important stories, including the story of the Samaritan woman, in the form of a *chiasm*, which is also called *inverted parallelism*. Basically, the first unit of the story matches its last unit, the second unit matches the second-to-last unit, and so on. If the story has an even number of units, the primary message of the story is to be found in the first and last units. If the story has an odd number of units, the story's primary message is to be found in the middle unit.

We will find all these literary features of John's Gospel in the story of the Samaritan woman's encounter with Jesus.

The Story of the Samaritan Woman in Context

Preceding this story about the Samaritan woman, the narrator tells us that Jesus was in Jerusalem for Passover (John 2:23). While there, he meets Nicodemus, and they have a conversation that ends with Jesus chiding Nicodemus for being a "teacher of Israel" who cannot understand what Jesus is saying (3:1-11). Jesus then turns away from Nicodemus and continues with a long discourse (interspersed with narrative) on heavenly and earthly things, salvation and condemnation, and baptism and eternal life (3:12-36). Finally, Jesus decides to leave Judea and return to Galilee when he hears that the Pharisees are receiving reports that he is becoming even more popular than John the Baptist (4:1-3).

This is where our story about the Samaritan woman begins. The opening sentence reads, "It was necessary that he pass through Samaria" (4:4, my translation). The use of the passive voice, where the subject is implied rather than directly stated, suggests that God is the one who is prompting Jesus to take this route back to Galilee. Ordinarily, Jews who needed to go from Judea to Galilee would simply cross the Jordan River and travel north on the east side of the river until they could cross the river again into Galilee. The reader who recognizes this literary convention as the divine passive will certainly wonder, "What does God intend to happen here in Samaria?"

 Like many stories in the Gospel of John, the story of the Samaritan Woman is arranged to convey **a deeper message beyond the literal sense** of the story. In this story, Jesus makes two commands that each lead to three exchanges between the woman and Jesus (4:7-15; 4:16-26). As the story concludes, we see two intertwined story lines, one involving Jesus' disciples who can best be described as confused, and the other involving a female outsider who gives witness to Jesus so that her compatriots come to believe in him. Who in this story is the most effective disciple?

For those who know the Hebrew Scriptures, the mention of Jesus sitting at the well is evocative of intimate encounters between men and women. Abraham's servant, who was sent to find a wife for Isaac, encountered Rebekah at a well and brought her home to Isaac (Gen 24:1-66). Jacob met his future wife Rachel at a well (Gen 29:1-11), and Moses met his soon-to-be wife, Zipporah, at a well (Exod 2:15-22). This is not to say that Jesus intended to marry this woman. Rather, we should consider that John is painting a scenario of profound and heartfelt encounter that breaks some of the most deeply embedded social norms of the time—namely, the animosity between Jews and Samaritans and the separation of men and women—for the sake of divine revelation to the world.

The narrator of this story tells us that the time of Jesus' encounter with the Samaritan woman takes place at "about noon" (4:6)—literally, "in the sixth hour." Only a foolish or desperate woman would go out to draw water at this hottest time of the day, but neither descriptor applies to John's portrait of the Samaritan woman. Instead, John is applying the literary

John 4:4-42

The Samaritan Woman. ⁴He had to pass through Samaria. ⁵So he came to a town of Samaria called Sychar, near the plot of land that Jacob had given to his son Joseph. ⁶Jacob's well was there. Jesus, tired from his journey, sat down there at the well. It was about noon.

⁷A woman of Samaria came to draw water. Jesus said to her, "Give me a drink." ⁸His disciples had gone into the town to buy food. ⁹The Samaritan woman said to him, "How can you, a Jew, ask me, a Samaritan woman, for a drink?" (For Jews use nothing in common with Samaritans.) ¹⁰Jesus answered and said to her, "If you knew the gift of God and who is saying to you, 'Give me a drink,' you would have asked him and he would have given you living water." ¹¹[The woman] said to him, "Sir, you do not even have a bucket and the well is deep; where then can you get this living water? ¹²Are you greater than our father Jacob, who gave us this well and drank from it himself with his children and his flocks?" ¹³Jesus answered and said to her, "Everyone who drinks this water will be thirsty again; ¹⁴but whoever drinks the water I shall give will never thirst; the water I shall give will become in him a spring of water welling up to eternal life." ¹⁵The woman said to him, "Sir, give me this water, so that I may not be thirsty or have to keep coming here to draw water."

¹⁶Jesus said to her, "Go call your husband and come back." ¹⁷The woman answered and said to him, "I do not have a husband." Jesus answered her, "You are right in saying, 'I do not have a husband.' ¹⁸For you have had five husbands, and the one you have now is not your husband. What you have said is true." ¹⁹The woman said to him, "Sir, I can see that you are a prophet. ²⁰Our ancestors worshiped on this mountain; but you people say that the place to worship is in Jerusalem." ²¹Jesus said to her, "Believe me, woman, the hour is coming when you will worship the Father neither on this mountain nor in Jerusalem. ²²You people worship what you do not understand; we worship what we understand,

continue

because salvation is from the Jews. ²³But the hour is coming, and is now here, when true worshipers will worship the Father in Spirit and truth; and indeed the Father seeks such people to worship him. ²⁴God is Spirit, and those who worship him must worship in Spirit and truth." ²⁵The woman said to him, "I know that the Messiah is coming, the one called the Anointed; when he comes, he will tell us everything." ²⁶Jesus said to her, "I am he, the one who is speaking with you."

²⁷At that moment his disciples returned, and were amazed that he was talking with a woman, but still no one said, "What are you looking for?" or "Why are you talking with her?" ²⁸The woman left her water jar and went into the town and said to the people, ²⁹"Come see a man who told me everything I have done. Could he possibly be the Messiah?" ³⁰They went out of the town and came to him. ³¹Meanwhile, the disciples urged him, "Rabbi, eat." ³²But he said to them, "I have food to eat of which you do not know." ³³So the disciples said to one another, "Could someone have brought him something to eat?" ³⁴Jesus said to them, "My food is to do the will of the one who sent me and to finish his work. ³⁵Do you not say, 'In four months the harvest will be here'? I tell you, look up and see the fields ripe for the harvest. ³⁶The reaper is already receiving his payment and gathering crops for eternal life, so that the sower and reaper can rejoice together. ³⁷For here the saying is verified that 'One sows and another reaps.' ³⁸I sent you to reap what you have not worked for; others have done the work, and you are sharing the fruits of their work."

³⁹Many of the Samaritans of that town began to believe in him because of the word of the woman who testified, "He told me everything I have done." ⁴⁰When the Samaritans came to him, they invited him to stay with them; and he stayed there two days. ⁴¹Many more began to believe in him because of his word, ⁴²and they said to the woman, "We no longer believe because of your word; for we have heard for ourselves, and we know that this is truly the savior of the world."

technique of dualism. Nicodemus comes to see Jesus at night, and Jesus leaves him in his disbelief or refusal to accept Jesus (3:1-11). However, Jesus encounters this woman at the brightest point of the day, and as the story unfolds, we discover that she becomes an evangelist, drawing others to believe in Jesus.

We can divide this rather lengthy story into three scenes. The first two scenes involve conversations between the Samaritan woman and Jesus. Such dialogue in itself was dangerous activity, as stated by Rabbi Jose ben Johanan and recorded in *Mishnah Pirke Aboth* 1:5: " 'Talk not much with womankind.' They say this of a man's wife; how much more of his fellow's wife. Hence the Sages have said, 'He that talks much with womankind brings evil upon himself.' " The third scene focuses on the action of the woman as juxtaposed with the confusion and lack of understanding of Jesus' disciples.

Scene One (4:7-15). Jesus' first words to the Samaritan woman are a command: "Give me a drink" (4:7). This directive introduces three brief exchanges between the woman and Jesus. Again, notice the sarcasm with which she responds: "How can you, a Jew, ask me, a Samaritan woman, for a drink?" (4:9). She knows the impact of Jewish prejudice against Samaritans, but we can imagine that she is further irritated by the audacity of this Jewish male who is making a demand of her in her own homeland, no less.

Jesus' response is cryptic but important to our understanding of the larger message of this story. He wants her to open herself to two realities: (1) Jesus' true identity and (2) the gift that God is offering through him. If she already understood these things, Jesus says, she would have said to *him*, "Give me a drink." He goes on to talk about "living water," which she understands in simple terms to mean a spring-fed well (4:10). Thus, she responds with another extremely sarcastic statement about her people possessing Jacob's well as part of their identity, while he lacks even the most basic equipment to do women's work (4:11-12). Nowhere else in the Bible is Jacob's well mentioned, except by implication in Genesis 33:18-20, the story about Jacob establishing a town in Shechem. After all, you can't have a town without a well!

As noted earlier, the woman's rhetorical question asking if Jesus is greater than Jacob is a good example of John's use of irony. The grammatical structure of the question is such that any first-century Greek speaker would be prompted to say in reply, "Certainly not!" But the community of John's Gospel would have noted the irony and would have replied, "Yes, indeed, Jesus really *is* greater than Jacob!"

Jesus goes on to clarify that the kind of living water he will provide will spring up inside of its recipient like a fountain (Greek *pégé*), producing eternal life. Most likely, this is a reference to the fullness of life that results from the outflowing of the Holy Spirit, which Jesus bequeaths on his followers before his death (John 16:4b-15; see also 3:5 and 7:38).

Notice also that this longer dialogue between Jesus and the Samaritan woman is an example of John's use of double meaning ("living water"), followed by misunderstanding (spring-fed well), and moving toward Jesus' clarifying expansion (life-giving abundance that Jesus will provide) to advance the story's message.

Still the woman does not understand. She asks again for physical water to quench her thirst and relieve her of the need to come to the well for water. The reader knows that Nicodemus did not understand Jesus' words either. Why did Jesus shut down the dialogue with Nicodemus, who went on misunderstanding Jesus, but continue to engage the Samaritan woman? Good question!

Scene Two (4:16-26). To the woman's repeated request for living water, Jesus responds with a second command: "Go away, call your husband/man, and come back here" (4:16, my translation). Observe the use of not one but three action verbs in this statement (*go, call, come*). This is an emphatic call to action.

Jesus' command initiates another three-part dialogue. When the woman says that she has no husband, Jesus affirms that she is telling the truth and elaborates on her words

by saying that she has had five husbands in the past and that the man she is with now is not her husband. In the history of interpretation of the Samaritan woman's story, people have concluded that this woman was a person of ill repute. They said that she must have been sexually promiscuous and that, out of shame, she came to the well in the middle of the day, when other women would have returned to their homes. But these interpreters fail to recognize that the timing of Jesus' encounter with the Samaritan woman "around noon" has symbolic purpose in John's larger narrative. Jesus does not offer even a hint of condemnation toward this woman, and the woman expresses no shame at his revelation. Instead, because of it, she perceives that he is a prophet.

 The reference to the Samaritan woman's **"five husbands"** as well as one who is **"not [her] husband"** is a confusing element of this story. We should probably assume that Samaritans followed the same practice of marriage and divorce as their Jewish counterparts. Only the husband had the right of divorce. Thus, we might say that this woman was incredibly unlucky to be widowed or divorced five times. Each successive marriage would have become harder and harder to arrange because fathers of eligible men might think something was wrong with this woman!

The person Jesus describes as "not your husband" might have been a wealthy patriarch who needed many servants to maintain his household. Regardless of how we interpret this detail, it must be noted that Jesus does not condemn her, nor does she perceive his comments to be a condemnation.

Observe also how theologically astute this woman is. She quickly takes advantage of this opportunity to ask Jesus about one of the major questions that separated Samaritans and Jews:

Lesson Three

Where should they worship? Jesus' response is interesting. First, he addresses her using the word "woman" (4:21), a term he also uses to address his mother in 2:4 and 19:26, and Mary Magdalene in 20:13-15. Is this significant in some way or simply a stylistic preference of the author? Second, he catches her attention by saying "Believe me" (4:21). Is this similar to the phrase "Amen, amen, I say to you," which is used multiple times in John's Gospel to signal that what Jesus is about to say is very important (e.g., 1:51; 3:3, 5, 11; 5:19, 24, 25)? Or is this a third command of Jesus to the Samaritan woman, this time to solicit a commitment of faith in him? The text is unclear on these questions.

The image below shows a model of the Second Temple in Jerusalem. The innermost **structure of the temple** is the Holy of Holies. The courtyard immediately surrounding it is the court of the men, and the courtyard just inside the walls is the court of the women. The outermost courtyard is the court of the Gentiles.

What is clear in this second exchange between the Samaritan woman and Jesus is that Jesus envisions a time in the near future when the physical location of worship for these two peoples—who share the same belief that they are God's chosen ones but who are enemies—will no longer matter. Instead, Jesus tells her, true or authentic worshipers "will worship the Father in Spirit and truth; and indeed the Father seeks such people to worship him" (4:23). The phrase "in Spirit and truth" is an example of a *hendiadys*, a figure of speech in which two words connected by "and" are used to express a single idea. Here it means something like "in the Spirit, which is where truth originates." Jesus adds that "God is Spirit" (4:24). In Jesus' answer to the Samaritan woman's question, therefore, we are to conclude that Jews and Samaritans will one day engage in worship that is performed "in the Spirit." What an amazing statement of inclusion, and on a much deeper and more profound level than physical location!

Pay attention, also, to this woman's persistence in pursuing her theological inquiry. Having heard Jesus' response to her question

about whether it is better to worship in Jerusalem or on Mount Gerizim, she is curious to know if he might be the messiah, but she does not ask directly. Instead, she acknowledges her belief in a messiah who, when he comes, will reveal all things (4:25). Something similar is said of Jesus in the prologue of this Gospel: "No one has ever seen God. The only Son, God, who is at the Father's side, has revealed him" (1:18). Jesus recognizes her veiled question and responds with the words *egó eimi* ("I am") or "I am (he), the (one) who is speaking to you" (4:26, my translation). This Greek phrase *egó eimi* is akin to the Hebrew *haya* (also transliterated as *hayah* or *éh-yeh*), meaning "I am" or NABRE: "I am who I am," the name God gave to Moses when Moses asked for God's name at the burning bush (Exod 3:13-14).

Notice how the woman's attitude toward Jesus is softening and how Jesus' true identity is coming to light as their conversation proceeds. First, she calls him "a Jew" (4:9), making clear that he is an outsider. Next, she calls him "Sir" (4:11, 15, 19; Greek *kurios*), which is a respectful form of address. Then she supposes that he is a prophet (4:19). Now Jesus confirms her suspicions that he is the messiah (meaning "anointed one") and the "I am" of God (4:25-26). The early Christian believers who were hearing this Gospel likely recognized Jesus' "I am" as a sign of his divinity. Did the Samaritan woman also understand?

Scene Three (4:27-42). The next segment in this extended narrative is especially interesting because it juxtaposes two events that are taking place at the same time. One is Jesus' encounter with the disciples, who have returned from their shopping trip (4:8, 27). They wonder why he has been talking to a woman, but they are afraid to ask. When they try to get Jesus to eat the food they brought for him, Jesus responds, "I have food to eat of which you do not know" (4:32). They talk among themselves about who might have given him food, but again they do not ask Jesus to explain. Meanwhile, the Samaritan woman has dropped her water jar, signaling that she has chosen a new mission

for herself, without prompting by Jesus, and has gone into the town (4:28). With the phrase "Come [and] see" (4:29), the Samaritan woman invites everyone she meets to discipleship with Jesus. This phrase ("Come [and] see") echoes earlier calls to discipleship within the Gospel: Jesus' invitation to Andrew and another person to follow him (1:39), and Philip's call to Nathanael to meet Jesus (1:46).

In making this invitation to "Come [and] see," the Samaritan woman calls attention to Jesus' ability to know and reveal even her private thoughts and activities. She adds, "He is not the messiah, is he?" (4:29, my translation). This question is somewhat confusing because it begins with the Greek word *méti*, which indicates that the answer should be negative, as in "No, he cannot be!" And yet she is inviting others to "Come [and] see," suggesting a call to discipleship. Is she also looking for reassurance from her neighbors? But without hesitation, the people leave the city to encounter Jesus for themselves and declare him to be "the savior of the world" (4:29-30, 42). This scene confirms what the Gospel prologue asserts: as the Word of God, Jesus is the revealer of God to all peoples (1:18)!

Returning to the dialogue between Jesus and the disciples, Jesus makes a cryptic statement about the end-time harvest of God's people: " 'One sows and another reaps.' I sent you to reap what you have not worked for; others have done the work, and you are sharing the fruits of their work" (4:37-38). But who is doing the sowing? The Samaritan woman! Against a persistent thread within the history of interpretation that has painted her as an outcast, a sinner, or a woman of ill repute, she is indeed the witness and evangelist, the announcer of good news, to the Samaritans on Jesus' behalf (4:39). And after hearing Jesus' words for themselves, the people respond, "[W]e know that this is truly the savior of the world" (4:42).

Although the New Testament makes several references to Jesus as saving all peoples, the title "savior of the world" appears only here in John's Gospel and in 1 John 4:14. Elsewhere, outside of the New Testament, the term "savior" was used of gods and heroes who provided their constituents rescue from difficult situations. For example, in the first century and into the second century CE, some form of this title was attributed to Roman emperors, from Julius Caesar to Augustus through Nero and beyond. The exact title "savior of the world" was attributed to Emperor Hadrian (reigned 117–138 CE). Was the author of the Gospel of John trying to make a political statement by asserting that Jesus is the Savior of the World?

Looking Again at the Whole Story

After analyzing the story of the Samaritan woman in detail, it is important that we not lose sight of its central message. Let's go back to the Samaritan woman's response to Jesus' request for a drink at the beginning of the story: "How can you, a Jew, ask me, a Samaritan woman, for a drink?" (4:9). And recall Jesus' reply: "If you knew the gift of God and who is saying to you, 'Give me a drink,' you would have asked him and he would have given you living water" (4:10). Recall that the Gospel writer is revealing two essential realities through this woman's story: (1) Jesus' true identity and (2) the gift that God is offering through him.

Concerning the first reality, Jesus' true identity, the Samaritan woman does not arrive at clear recognition or full faith in Jesus all at once. Rather, she progresses through a series of steps until, finally, she and her Samaritan neighbors are able to proclaim Jesus as Savior of the World. Here are the steps of her faith journey, described in terms of attributions given to Jesus:

- A Jew (intended negatively)

- Sir (a social convention; signal of respect)

- A prophet (a spokesperson of God)

- Messiah (the "Anointed" of God)

- The "I am" of God

- The Savior of the World!

Later in the Gospel, John 9:1-41 contains a similar story in which the central character progresses toward a full recognition of Jesus' identity. The central character is a man who was blind from birth. After Jesus heals him, the man witnesses to Jesus' identity through a series of encounters with his neighbors and the Jewish religious authorities. Hopefully both of these stories prompt us to reflect on our own journeys toward full recognition of Jesus' identity. Both stories can also be a source of encouragement to remain faithful to the journey. Persistence builds courage to take up the call to authentic evangelization and action that the Gospel demands of us.

The second reality that the story of the Samaritan woman reveals—the gift of God that is being offered to us—is perhaps best understood by looking at the chiasm that forms the structure of the story. Chiasms are not easy for modern readers to recognize because we do not often use this literary convention today, and because chiasms are easier to spot in their original Greek language than in our English translations. However, the first recipients of this story likely would have noticed the chiasm immediately as they heard the pattern of the story fold back on itself.

This is an odd-numbered chiasm, as shown in the following outline:

A. The Samaritan woman encounters Jesus (4:4-9)

  B. Jesus provides a teaching on living water (4:10-15)

    C. Jesus witnesses about the Samaritan woman (4:16-19)

      D. Jesus provides a teaching on true worship (4:20-26)

    C'. The Samaritan woman witnesses about Jesus (4:27-30)

  B'. Jesus provides a teaching about true food (4:31-38)

A'. Samaritans encounter Jesus (4:39-42)

In a chiasm, the first and last units share similarities. Likewise, the second and second-to-last units and the third and third-to-last units share similarities. Because this is an odd-numbered chiasm, the central message that the Gospel writer wants to convey can be found in the middle unit. What is the gift of God that is offered to the Samaritan woman—and to us? Jesus, the Messiah and the "I am" of God, offers us "living water" that springs up to eternal life (i.e., fullness of life) so that humanity, regardless of differing religious traditions, can worship the Father in Spirit and truth. Praise God for this amazing gift!

The Woman Caught in Adultery

Another important exchange between Jesus and a woman in John's Gospel is the account of a woman caught in the act of adultery (7:53–8:11). Before being included in the final form of John's Gospel, this account might have circulated as a distinct story independent of the Gospel for a time. Scholars suspect this because it appears to interrupt the flow of John 7–8 (known as the Tabernacles Discourse) and because the style of writing in this story is very different from John's other stories.

The narrator tells us that the scribes and Pharisees brought this woman to Jesus for judgment, and Jesus responded, "Let the one among you who is without sin be the first to throw a stone at her" (John 8:7). Gradually everyone walked away, leaving the woman and Jesus alone in the temple area.

Clearly, the religious authorities were setting a trap for Jesus. But how did they know that this woman was engaged in adultery? It took two male witnesses to make such charges stick. Were they spying on her? Did they lie about what they saw? Was Jesus aware of her dilemma and therefore chose not to condemn her? While we may never know the original context of this story, it should remind us that a person who appears to be guilty of wrongdoing might actually be a victim who is worthy of Jesus' protection and care.

EXPLORING LESSON THREE

1. To better appreciate the tension between the Samaritan woman and Jesus in the opening scene of this story (John 4:7-15), think of two groups of people today who have deeply rooted hostilities toward each other. How do their strong negative judgments manifest in their dealings with the other group? What typically happens when individuals get to know one another personally? How does this insight impact the way you interpret John's story of the Samaritan woman?

_____

_____

_____

_____

_____

_____

_____

2. How would you describe the Samaritan woman's personality based on a careful reading of the first scene of the story (John 4:7-15)? What do you like or dislike about her? How does your perception of her change in scene three (John 4:27-42)?

_____

_____

_____

_____

_____

_____

3. Apply what you know about the dualism of light and darkness in John's Gospel to explain the symbolic meaning behind this encounter happening "about noon" (John 4:6).

_____

_____

_____

_____

_____

_____

_____

4. Reflect on the following statement of Jesus: "Everyone who drinks this water will be thirsty again; but whoever drinks the water I shall give will never thirst; the water I shall give will become in him a spring of water welling up to eternal life" (John 4:13-14). What does this verse mean to you? How do you experience this outflowing of the Holy Spirit in your everyday life?

_____

_____

_____

_____

_____

_____

_____

5. At the beginning of scene three of this story (John 4:27-42), the narrator indicates that the Samaritan woman left behind her water jar as she returned to her village. Biblical scholars have long debated the significance of this detail in the story. What do you make of it? If she was going home, why did she leave the water jar behind?

_____

_____

_____

_____

_____

_____

_____

6. Compare the description of Jesus' disciples with the activity of the Samaritan woman in scene three (John 4:27-42). Metaphorically speaking, who is best described as "walking in the light"?

_____

_____

_____

_____

_____

_____

_____

_____

7. Reflect on the progression of titles of Jesus (e.g., "Sir" and "Messiah") that appear in this story. What patterns do you see in the way these titles are presented? What, if anything, does it say about how someone comes to faith in Jesus Christ?

_____

_____

_____

_____

_____

_____

8. According to the structure of this story, its central message can be found in response to the woman's curiosity about whether Samaritan or Jewish practices are the correct way to worship God (John 4:20). Jesus says true worshipers will worship God "in Spirit and truth," that is, through the Spirit who is the source of truth (4:23-24). What meaning might these words have for today's Christians who sometimes find themselves at odds with other Christians about the correct way to worship God and live their faith?

_____

_____

_____

_____

_____

_____

9. This lesson has provided a close reading of one story from John's Gospel. What was your experience of doing this close reading? What was your main takeaway from the story of Jesus and the Samaritan woman at the well?

_____

_____

_____

_____

_____

_____

CLOSING PRAYER

Prayer

"Come see a man who told me everything I have done. Could he possibly be the Messiah?"
(John 4:29)

Gracious and loving God, we thank you for the witness of the Samaritan woman who encountered Jesus at a well in Samaritan territory and began a journey of discovery into the fullness of Jesus' identity. Like her, may we evangelize with such genuineness that those we meet are attracted to you and your son Jesus, who is Savior of the World. Inspired by this woman of faith, we pray today especially for . . .

LESSON FOUR

Mary and Martha, Models of Devotion and Service

Begin your personal study and group discussion with a simple and sincere prayer such as:

Prayer

God of love and consolation, as we study the women of the New Testament, open our hearts and minds to appreciate the unique gifts they each brought to their faith communities. May their witness inspire us today to use the gifts we have received in service of your holy ones.

Read pages 64–75, Lesson Four, highlighting what stands out to you.

Respond to the questions on pages 76–78, Exploring Lesson Four.

The Closing Prayer on page 79 is for your personal use and may be used at the end of group discussion.

MARY AND MARTHA, MODELS OF DEVOTION AND SERVICE

Most Christians know at least something about the story of Mary and Martha, a story that is often cited in homilies and Bible studies as an instruction on the value of the contemplative life, in which we are invited to sit at Jesus' feet and prayerfully listen to his teachings.

It is less commonly known that the story of Martha serving and Mary sitting at the feet of Jesus (Luke 10:38-42) is just one of several Gospel stories about two people named Mary and Martha. The other stories are found in John's Gospel, though it is unclear whether Luke's Mary and Martha are the same people as John's Mary and Martha. To make this investigation even more complicated, in the history of interpretation of the stories of Mary and Martha, these women (Mary in particular) have often been collapsed into the story of the woman who washes and anoints Jesus' feet at a banquet (Luke 7:36-50), the story of the woman who anoints Jesus' head in preparation for his burial (Matt 26:6-13; Mark 14:3-9), and even the story of Mary Magdalene. Unfortunately, the tradition also misidentifies Mary and Martha as repentant sinners.

Let us look now at what the biblical texts actually tell us about these women.

Mary and Martha in Luke's Gospel

We will begin with Luke's account of Jesus' encounter with Mary and Martha in their home:

Luke 10:38-42

Martha and Mary. [38]As they [Jesus and his disciples] continued their journey he entered a village where a woman whose name was Martha welcomed him. [39]She had a sister named Mary [who] sat beside the Lord at his feet listening to him speak. [40]Martha, burdened with much serv-

---

ing, came to him and said, "Lord, do you not care that my sister has left me by myself to do the serving? Tell her to help me." [41]The Lord said to her in reply, "Martha, Martha, you are anxious and worried about many things. [42]There is need of only one thing. Mary has chosen the better part and it will not be taken from her."

Immediately preceding this story in Luke's Gospel is the parable of the good Samaritan (10:29-37), which is about right observance of Jewish law and what it means to love one's neighbor. Immediately following the story about Mary and Martha is Jesus' teaching on how to pray, including the words of what we now call the Lord's Prayer (11:1-4).

Luke's story notes that these two women are sisters, but it does not tell us where their village is located. Previous mentions of geographic locations in Luke's Gospel are Bethsaida on the north shore of the Sea of Galilee (9:10) and an unnamed Samaritan village that Jesus passes through on his way to Jerusalem (9:51-52). Luke does not describe Jesus entering Jerusalem until much later in his narrative (19:28). Thus, according to Luke's chronology, the place where Jesus encounters Mary and

Martha is somewhere between an unnamed Samaritan village and Jerusalem in Judea. This detail is important to note when tackling the question of whether the Mary and Martha of Luke's Gospel are the same Mary and Martha that we find in John's Gospel.

The Greek text of Luke's story about Mary and Martha raises many questions and opportunities for interpretation. For example, Luke makes no mention of male relatives or spouses associated with Mary and Martha. Therefore, we might assume that Martha is widowed or unmarried, especially since she is the one who "welcome[s]" Jesus (Greek *hupodechomai*, meaning "to receive someone as a guest" or "to entertain hospitably"). Ordinarily, this welcoming or receiving would be the privilege and task of the male head of the household. Is this, then, Martha's home and not the home of her father, husband, or brother? Some ancient manuscripts add "into the house" or "into her house" after "Martha welcomed him" (10:38). (Remember that we do not have originals of any of the New Testament books, only copies of copies that have been researched extensively to establish the best possible reconstruction of the original text.)

The next sentence of the story is translated here as "She had a sister named Mary [who] sat beside the Lord at his feet" (10:39). However, the Greek conjunction *kai*, meaning "and" or "also," is used in this sentence immediately before the phrase "sat beside the Lord at his feet." Thus, we could read this portion of the text to mean that both women had been sitting at Jesus' feet listening to his words, but Martha was distracted (Greek *periespato*, meaning "to be drawn away, troubled, or distressed") by the many expectations of

hospitality, hence her request to have Jesus tell Mary to help her with the serving. Jesus then speaks her name twice, perhaps to capture her attention and bring her out of her frustrated state. He goes on to name her emotions, perhaps as a way of calming her, and adds that there is "need of only one thing" (10:42).

This interpretation of 10:42 reflects the manuscript evidence that the NABRE uses in its translation. However, there are other early manuscripts that have a different reading: "Martha, Martha, you are anxious and worried about many things, but few things are necessary—*or really only one.*" This longer version was known among early church writers, and at least a few took it to mean that Martha was doing too much. That is, she need not prepare so many dishes—and perhaps no more

than one—to properly entertain Jesus in her home. In today's vernacular, Jesus might say, "Please, Martha, stop your worrying and come sit down with us. This one dish of food is more than enough."

There is one more detail in this story that warrants our attention because it has the potential to change how we think about its message. In the ancient world, sitting at the feet of the master or teacher was understood to be the position of discipleship—the Greek word for "disciple" literally means "learner"—and was generally reserved for men. Young women from well-to-do families might have received an academic education if their fathers so chose, but seldom in the presence of other male students. They also had to conduct themselves in ways that did not call attention to their academic abilities so as not to imply that their intellectual proficiency was greater than or equal to that of their male counterparts. But here, the Lukan Jesus invites and encourages these two women to engage in discipleship without restrictions. Mary has already chosen the better part, Jesus says, and Martha can do the same, if she is willing to let go of her anxiety and worry over the details of hospitality—traditionally women's work—and return to simply *listening* to his words as a disciple.

As noted above, Luke's story of Mary and Martha is not found in the other two Synoptic Gospels (Matthew and Mark). Biblical scholars have long been aware that John's Gospel contains stories about two characters known by the same names, which raises questions about whether the author of John's Gospel knew of or had read Luke's Gospel (or vice versa). As we have already noted, Luke's Gospel is vague about the location of Jesus' encounter with Mary and Martha, and there is no mention of a brother named Lazarus. The Gospel of John states that these two women encounter Jesus in their home village of Bethany, approximately two miles from Jerusalem, and that they are sisters of Lazarus and friends of Jesus.

Today, after years of investigation into the question of literary dependence, it is generally accepted that the Gospel of John was written independently of the Synoptic Gospels. That is, the author of John's Gospel was not reading Luke's story about Mary and Martha and adapting it for his purposes, or vice versa. However, it is less clear whether the Mary and Martha in John's Gospel are different people from the Mary and Martha in Luke's Gospel. For example, it is possible that John knew about these two women from oral traditions. At the same time, these two Gospels do not share enough detail about Mary and Martha to say definitively that we are reading about the same sisters. Our approach, then, will be to leave this question unsolved, which means we will not be comparing Luke's and John's stories about Mary and Martha but rather treating them separately to further our appreciation of women's roles in the life of Jesus.

 Early New Testament Manuscripts

Prior to the invention of the Gutenberg printing press in the fifteenth century, copies of the Bible were handwritten, which is why we call these early versions "manuscripts," from the Latin terms *manu* ("by hand") and *scriptus* ("written").

None of the original copies of New Testament books exist today. However, we know of nearly 6,000 Greek manuscripts or fragments of manuscripts of the New Testament. Biblical scholars gather, date, and compare these manuscripts to reconstruct as closely as possible the original text of the Bible.

This painstaking work is done before the biblical book is translated into English. However, if you have a study Bible, you may occasionally see notes indicating something like: "Other ancient authorities read . . ." This is how biblical scholars signal to the reader that there is more than one credible option for the original text.

John's Story of the Raising of Lazarus

The Gospel of John contains two stories about Mary and Martha: the raising of Lazarus (11:1-44) and the anointing of Jesus (12:1-11). We will begin with the story of the raising of Lazarus, the brother of Mary and Martha. This story is best categorized as an extended miracle story. The first element of a miracle story is the description of the problem: "So the sisters sent word to him, saying, 'Master, the one you love is ill'" (11:3). However, the second and third elements of a miracle story—the miracle worker's word or deed and evidence that the miracle took place—are not recounted until very near the end of the story (see 11:43-44).

Moreover, John's Gospel contains seven miracle stories, which the Gospel writer calls "signs." Seven is a symbolic number, representing fullness or perfection, and we should think of the author's "signs" as pointing toward something. The raising of Lazarus is the seventh and last sign of this Gospel. The author of the Gospel uses it to confirm the religious authorities' resolve to arrest Jesus and put him to death (11:45-53).

John's account of the raising of Lazarus uses many of the same literary features that we saw in the story of the Samaritan woman (John 4:4-42). Also, the carefully crafted structure of this story suggests that the author of this Gospel is doing something more than simply preserving an early tradition of Jesus' miracle-working. Rather, he has embedded within this account a profound theological message. The outline provided will help us navigate the complexities of this story.

Setting and introduction of characters; miracle requested but delayed (11:1-6)

As noted above, Lazarus is described here as the brother of Mary and Martha (11:2). Bethany, the village in which they reside, is described as "the village of Mary and her sister Martha" rather than "the village of Lazarus," as we would expect in a patriarchal society (11:1). This emphasis on Mary and Martha over Lazarus may indicate that these two women were of higher social status in the community than their brother or that they were well respected in the village. The narrator explains that Jesus loved all three—Martha, Mary, and Lazarus—but notice the order in which they are named. We would expect the narrator to say "Lazarus and his two sisters" instead of naming each of the three separately and placing the women's names before Lazarus's name. Is the Gospel writer signaling that our attention ought to be placed on Jesus' interaction with these two women more than on Lazarus? The narrator also provides a "flash forward" to the next chapter of the Gospel by saying that this Mary is the same one who later anoints Jesus' feet at a banquet that these two women provide in honor of Jesus and their brother (see John 12:1-8).

Preceding this story about the raising of Lazarus, the narrator places Jesus and his disciples in the area where John the Baptist had been baptizing (John 10:40). While we do not know the exact site today, we can estimate that it was some twenty miles from Jerusalem, which would have been a full day's journey for someone who was physically fit and trained for walking. Thus, it would have taken a messenger at least a day to locate Jesus and his disciples and another day for them to walk to Bethany. But the narrator notes that Jesus decides to wait for two days before leaving. Why? "This illness is not to

---

John 11:1-53

The Raising of Lazarus. ¹Now a man was ill, Lazarus from Bethany, the village of Mary and her sister Martha. ²Mary was the one who had anointed the Lord with perfumed oil and dried his feet with her hair; it was her brother Lazarus who was ill. ³So the sisters sent word to him, saying, "Master, the one you love is ill." ⁴When Jesus heard this he said, "This illness is not to end in death, but is for the glory of God, that the Son of God may be glorified through it." ⁵Now Jesus loved Martha and her sister and Lazarus. ⁶So when he heard that he was ill, he remained for two days in the place where he was.

continue

⁷Then after this he said to his disciples, "Let us go back to Judea." ⁸The disciples said to him, "Rabbi, the Jews were just trying to stone you, and you want to go back there?" ⁹Jesus answered, "Are there not twelve hours in a day? If one walks during the day, he does not stumble, because he sees the light of this world. ¹⁰But if one walks at night, he stumbles, because the light is not in him." ¹¹He said this, and then told them, "Our friend Lazarus is asleep, but I am going to awaken him." ¹²So the disciples said to him, "Master, if he is asleep, he will be saved." ¹³But Jesus was talking about his death, while they thought that he meant ordinary sleep. ¹⁴So then Jesus said to them clearly, "Lazarus has died. ¹⁵And I am glad for you that I was not there, that you may believe. Let us go to him." ¹⁶So Thomas, called Didymus, said to his fellow disciples, "Let us also go to die with him."

end in death, but is for the glory of God, that the Son of God may be glorified through it" (11:4). As a preview to the rest of the story, we should be reminded that, in John's Gospel, the notion of Jesus' glorification is closely tied to his death and exaltation, which is his return to the Father.

Jesus talks to his disciples about going to Judea (11:7-16)

Presumably, the disciples are present to hear Jesus' words about Lazarus's illness (11:4), but it is clear that they do not understand, because in this segment of the story, they seem clueless when Jesus talks about Lazarus having fallen asleep (11:13). But having the narrator give voice to these words allows the reader—you and I—to know and understand the significance of this story. Jesus further emphasizes his purposeful delay when he says to the disciples, "And I am glad for you that I was not there, that you may believe" (11:15).

Setting and introduction of characters; **miracle requested but delayed** (11:1-6)

Jesus talks to his disciples about going to Judea (11:7-16)
a) Jesus tells the disciples, "Let us go back to Judea" (11:7)
b) A dialogue about Lazarus's death (11:8-14)
c) Jesus and his disciples depart (11:15-16)

Jesus meets and talks with Martha (11:17-27)
a) Jesus comes (11:17, 20a)
b) Mourners are present (11:18-19)
c) Martha goes to meet Jesus (11:20b)
d) Martha says, "Lord, if you had been here" (11:21-22)
e) Dialogue (11:23-27)

Jesus meets and talks with Mary; Jesus raises Lazarus from the dead (11:28-44)
a) Jesus asks for Mary (11:28)
b) Mourners are present (11:30-31)
c) Mary goes to meet Jesus (11:29, 32a)
d) Mary says, "Lord, if you had been here" (11:32b)
e) Dialogue (11:33-42)
f) **Miracle effected and witnessed** (11:43-44)

Reaction to the miracle (11:45-53)
a) The people are divided (11:45-46)
b) Plot to kill Jesus (11:47-53)

Jesus meets and talks with Martha (11:17-27)

Jesus finally arrives in Bethany, a two-mile walk from Jerusalem. The narrator notes that many Jews are present, mourning with Mary and Martha, another indication of their high social status. Burials were conducted very soon after death because embalming was not commonly practiced in first-century Palestine. Women could participate in the funeral procession, though they walked separately from the men and then retired to the deceased person's family home to continue their mourning. Martha's act of going out to the edge of the village to meet Jesus is therefore striking. Going out to greet visitors was an activity that was ordinarily reserved for men, especially in the context of burial practices. Additionally, the Gospel writer appears to know the belief held by some first-century Jewish writers that the soul or spirit of the deceased hovered around the body for three days, hence the comment about Lazarus having been entombed for four days already when Jesus arrives (11:17). In other words, Lazarus is fully and irretrievably dead, and his body is rotting away!

The sad state of Lazarus's body is what prompts Martha and, later, Mary to say, "Lord, if you had been here, my brother would not have died" (11:21, 32). They knew Jesus to be a miracle worker, a folk healer with extraordinary gifts, but they also understood that only God could raise the dead. Yet Martha, at least, continues to affirm her belief in Jesus' special relationship with God such that God will give him whatever he asks (11:22). She also affirms belief in the resurrection of the dead at the end time (11:24), a position held by many of the Pharisees of the time and described in Daniel 12:1-3.

In response to these statements, Jesus says, "I am the resurrection and the life" (11:25). Martha answers him, "Yes, Lord. I always believed, and still do, that you are the Messiah, the Son of God, the one who is coming into the world" (11:27, my translation). In the original Greek, the verb "believe" is written in the present perfect tense, meaning it is a past, completed action whose results continue into the present ("always believed, and still do").

[17]When Jesus arrived, he found that Lazarus had already been in the tomb for four days. [18]Now Bethany was near Jerusalem, only about two miles away. [19]And many of the Jews had come to Martha and Mary to comfort them about their brother. [20]When Martha heard that Jesus was coming, she went to meet him; but Mary sat at home. [21]Martha said to Jesus, "Lord, if you had been here, my brother would not have died. [22][But] even now I know that whatever you ask of God, God will give you." [23]Jesus said to her, "Your brother will rise." [24]Martha said to him, "I know he will rise, in the resurrection on the last day." [25]Jesus told her, "I am the resurrection and the life; whoever believes in me, even if he dies, will live, [26]and everyone who lives and believes in me will never die. Do you believe this?" [27]She said to him, "Yes, Lord. I have come to believe that you are the Messiah, the Son of God, the one who is coming into the world."

[28]When she had said this, she went and called her sister Mary secretly, saying, "The teacher is here and is asking for you." [29]As soon as she heard this, she rose quickly and went to him. [30]For Jesus had not yet come into the village, but was still where Martha had met him. [31]So when the Jews who were with her in the house comforting her saw Mary get up quickly and go out, they followed her, presuming that she was going to the tomb to weep there. [32]When Mary came to where Jesus was and saw him, she fell at his

continue

The question before us is whether Martha really understands what Jesus has said to her. And does she fully understand what it means to call Jesus "the Son of God"?

Jesus meets and talks with Mary; Jesus raises Lazarus from the dead (11:28-44)

A very similar literary pattern unfolds as we learn that Mary now leaves the house and goes to the outskirts of the village to meet Jesus and make her complaint: "Lord, if you had been here, my brother would not have died" (11:32). Notice, however, that Mary falls at Jesus' feet,

feet and said to him, "Lord, if you had been here, my brother would not have died." [33]When Jesus saw her weeping and the Jews who had come with her weeping, he became perturbed and deeply troubled, [34]and said, "Where have you laid him?" They said to him, "Sir, come and see." [35]And Jesus wept. [36]So the Jews said, "See how he loved him." [37]But some of them said, "Could not the one who opened the eyes of the blind man have done something so that this man would not have died?"

[38]So Jesus, perturbed again, came to the tomb. It was a cave, and a stone lay across it. [39]Jesus said, "Take away the stone." Martha, the dead man's sister, said to him, "Lord, by now there will be a stench; he has been dead for four days." [40]Jesus said to her, "Did I not tell you that if you believe you will see the glory of God?" [41]So they took away the stone. And Jesus raised his eyes and said, "Father, I thank you for hearing me. [42]I know that you always hear me; but because of the crowd here

a gesture of petition or of worship. Also notice Jesus' reaction when he witnesses Mary and the Jews who were with her "weeping" (Greek *klaió*, meaning "to lament or to mourn"). The NABRE says that "he became perturbed and deeply troubled" (11:33), but a more literal translation might read, "In his spirit, he snorted as with anger and was agitated inwardly." That is a lot of emotion to hold in one's body! After Jesus asks where Lazarus has been interred, the narrator notes that "Jesus wept" (11:35). The Greek word *dakruó*, used here, is a synonym of *klaió*, but with the added connotation of shedding tears.

Why is Jesus grieving so intensely? Is it for Mary's sake, because of the loss of her brother, or for Lazarus, whom the sisters describe as the one Jesus loved (11:3)? Is it a response to the evil that is death? Or is it perhaps Jesus' response to what he knows will be the result of his raising of Lazarus (see 11:45-54)?

Mary does not speak further in this story. Does she go with the crowd who directed Jesus

to Lazarus's tomb, or does she return home? We do not know, but we do know that Martha is present at the tomb because she alerts Jesus to the state of Lazarus's body four days after his death (11:39). There is no hope of resuscitation, and by now the body would certainly be giving off the odor of a rotting corpse. Notice the words that Jesus directs toward Martha: "Did I not tell you that if you believe you will see the glory of God?" (11:40; cf. 11:4). What does this question tell us about Martha's proclamation of faith earlier in the story?

Pay attention, also, to Jesus' prayer to the Father (11:41-42). Although Jesus addresses the Father, his words are ultimately directed toward Martha and the others gathered at the tomb. What is the message that Jesus wants Martha to hear?

"The Jews" in John's Gospel

John's story of the raising of Lazarus includes a mention of Jews who came from Jerusalem to grieve with Mary and Martha (11:31, 36). They are presented here as empathetic and likeable characters, but the Greek phrase *hoi Ioudaioi*, translated here as "the Jews," is often used negatively as a blanket term for Jesus' opponents in John's Gospel.

Hoi Ioudaioi can also be translated as "Judeans" or "people of Judea," so some biblical scholars use this more neutral term in their commentaries. Most likely, the Gospel of John was written for a Jewish Christian audience that was locked in a bitter dispute with another group of Jews who did not accept Jesus as their messiah. This tension no doubt influences the use of the term "the Jews" throughout this Gospel.

Regardless of our interpretation of *hoi Ioudaioi*, we must be clear that there is no place for antisemitic hate in Christianity. Our Jewish brothers and sisters are our kinfolk in the faith and are forever God's chosen people.

Reaction to the miracle (11:45-53)

This story seems to end rather abruptly because we are not told about Mary's and Martha's reactions to the raising of their brother. In addition, the story ends on a somber and even troubling note because, after learning about this resuscitation, the chief priests and Pharisees in Jerusalem convene the Sanhedrin to figure out what they should do about Jesus. In the end, they concur with the high priest Caiaphas, who prophesies that it is better "that one man should die instead of the people, so that the whole nation may not perish" (11:50). Thus, the plot to kill Jesus is fully underway. While the high priest was probably concerned about a possible riot that would bring the Roman armies upon the city, early Christians likely recognized the irony of his prophecy. Jesus' death would bring about the salvation of all God's people, just not in the way they expect.

 The term **"resuscitation"** refers to the fact that Lazarus is brought back to life only temporarily. Eventually he will experience physical death like all of us. By contrast, the term "resurrection" is used of Jesus because he triumphs over death forever.

I have said this, that they may believe that you sent me." ⁴³And when he had said this, he cried out in a loud voice, "Lazarus, come out!" ⁴⁴The dead man came out, tied hand and foot with burial bands, and his face was wrapped in a cloth. So Jesus said to them, "Untie him and let him go."

Session of the Sanhedrin. ⁴⁵Now many of the Jews who had come to Mary and seen what he had done began to believe in him. ⁴⁶But some of them went to the Pharisees and told them what Jesus had done. ⁴⁷So the chief priests and the Pharisees convened the Sanhedrin and said, "What are we going to do? This man is performing many signs. ⁴⁸If we leave him alone, all will believe in him, and the Romans will come and take away both our land and our nation." ⁴⁹But one of them, Caiaphas, who was high priest that year, said to them, "You know nothing, ⁵⁰nor do you consider that it is better for you that one man should die instead of the people, so that the whole nation may not perish." ⁵¹He did not say this on his own, but since he was high priest for that year, he prophesied that Jesus was going to die for the nation, ⁵²and not only for the nation, but also to gather into one the dispersed children of God. ⁵³So from that day on they planned to kill him.

As we sum up our analysis of the story of the raising of Lazarus, you may have noticed that the theological message embedded in the story can be found in its dialogue sections. Martha, in particular, though in the presence of many mourners, becomes the recipient of a very important teaching about the glory of God and about Jesus being glorified through her brother's death and resuscitation (11:40; cf. 11:4). Twice she is invited to believe in him and, therefore, to walk in the light (11:26, 40). Martha will not stumble, because she can see the light of the world (11:9-10).

In contrast, Jesus' disciples walk in the darkness, as evidenced by the fact that they fail to understand what Jesus is saying about Lazarus's death (11:5-15). Thomas declares that he will go with Jesus to Judea so that he may die with him (11:16), but the narrator makes no mention of the disciples when Jesus arrives in Bethany. Where did they go? Instead, Martha stands as a symbol for all of us. How will we respond when Jesus says to us, "Did I not tell you that if you believe you will see the glory of God?" (11:40)?

John's Story of the Anointing of Jesus

Immediately after the story of the raising of Lazarus, the Gospel of John provides another story about Mary and Martha of Bethany. This time, Mary features more prominently than Martha.

John 12:1-11

The Anointing at Bethany. ¹Six days before Passover Jesus came to Bethany, where Lazarus was, whom Jesus had raised from the dead. ²They gave a dinner for him there, and Martha served, while Lazarus was one of those reclining at table with him. ³Mary took a liter of costly perfumed oil made from genuine aromatic nard and anointed the feet of Jesus and dried them with her hair; the house was filled with the fragrance of the oil. ⁴Then Judas the Iscariot, one [of] his disciples, and the one who would betray him, said, ⁵"Why was this oil not sold for three hundred days' wages and given to the poor?" ⁶He said this not because he cared about the poor but because he was a thief and held the money bag and used to steal the contributions. ⁷So Jesus said, "Leave her alone. Let her keep this for the day of my burial. ⁸You always have the poor with you, but you do not always have me."

⁹[The] large crowd of the Jews found out that he was there and came, not only because of Jesus, but also to see Lazarus, whom he had raised from the dead. ¹⁰And the chief priests plotted to kill Lazarus too, ¹¹because many of the Jews were turning away and believing in Jesus because of him.

The temporal setting of this story is "[s]ix days before Passover" (12:1). Some have attempted to read symbolism into this number six. However, the narrator has already indicated that Passover was "near" (11:55). Now it is so close that we can count the days! Since Passover was a seven-day pilgrimage feast, Jerusalem was probably already filling with visitors looking for places to stay, and Bethany, being less than two miles away, was likely affected by this influx of pilgrims as well.

Some biblical scholars have argued that the somewhat awkward mentions of Lazarus in verses 1-2 and 10-11 are an attempt by a later redactor (editor) to tie chapters 11 and 12 more closely together. However, since this issue is immaterial to our concern about Mary's role in the Gospel story, we will leave it unresolved except to say that we should not be surprised to see evidence of editorial work in ancient religious texts. Although we talk about biblical authors in the singular, these religious texts often are the product of a community's reflection on the traditions that were handed on to them.

As the story begins, Jesus has arrived at Mary and Martha's village for a banquet in his honor. It is not clear who arranged for the banquet, because the Greek verb *poieó* ("gave") is in the third-person plural and there is no reference to who "they" are. However, because the narrator indicates that Martha "served" (12:2), we can assume that the meal was at Martha's home and that Martha and Mary hosted it. To have a female host of a banquet would have been unusual except in a situation where there was no male head of household and where the woman was well-off and recognized to be of high social status.

 "Triclinium" is the name given to a dining room in an upper-class, first-century Roman home. The triclinium had a U-shaped arrangement of three couches or platforms with cushions for reclining at dinner, and inside edges of the platform or a small table in the middle on which food was placed in common bowls or platters. Places were assigned according to one's social status.

Likewise, a banquet in which participants reclined for the meal was usually only for men, but wealthy women of high social status might be given rein to break the rules of proper etiquette. Such was likely the case with Martha and Mary. Did these two women recline alongside the men, or were they seated on the outer edges of the triclinium? Although the practice of male-only banquets was already beginning to change in the first century CE, people who were accustomed to the old ways disapproved of men and women reclining at table together. Given their high social status in the community, these two women likely stationed themselves along the outer edges of the triclinium. This location would have made it easier for Martha to oversee the meal service by her household servants. It would also have made

it easier for Mary to be in position for her action on Jesus' behalf.

While the first courses of a banquet were being served, one of the household slaves would have performed the typical acts of hospitality: foot washing and anointing. In the first-century Mediterranean world, washing and anointing guests' feet had a practical purpose: people's feet were always dirty from walking the streets and country roads. But it was also a way of honoring your guests. Neglecting or deliberately choosing not to provide this service was a very public way of dishonoring a guest at your table.

Here is where the story takes a shocking turn. Assuming that Mary was seated on the outer edges of the triclinium, taking the role of a respectable woman, she finds herself in a position to personally minister to Jesus. Imagine the gasps coming from the partygoers as Mary takes on the work of a lowly slave to anoint Jesus' feet. In an even more scandalous act, Mary removes her head covering and takes down her hair so she can dry his feet with it. Certainly, she could afford a towel! Honorable women would not have displayed themselves in this way except for their husbands in the privacy of their homes, but here she is, exposing herself to considerable shame out of love for Jesus.

Not only does Mary take the position of a slave in order to perform this gesture of hospitality, but she is extremely generous in doing so. The Greek word *litra* (translated in 12:3 as "liter") is equivalent to a Roman pound. The two most popular conveyances used in perfume-making were olive oil and almond oil. A Roman pound of olive oil is 12.4 ounces in US liquid measure, and a Roman pound of almond oil is 17 ounces in liquid measure. Ancient Roman and Egyptian perfume jars that have survived to today come in many sizes and shapes, but the most common ones were made from blown glass; had long, narrow necks with small, rounded cavities at the bottom of the vessels; and were capable of holding only a few ounces of fluid. It would have taken an extremely large perfume bottle to hold as much costly perfume as is described in this story!

Mary of Bethany *by George William Joy*

Moreover, Mary uses the perfume so liberally that its fragrance fills the entire house.

The Gospels contain several versions of a story in which Jesus is anointed by a woman, raising the question of the **significance of anointing**. Olive oil was used for healing and cleansing or for purifying persons or objects, but anointing a person's head was usually reserved for the consecration of kings (e.g., 1 Sam 16), high priests (Ps 133:2), and prophets (Isa 61:1). The Greek word *chrio* means "to anoint," and *christos* means "anointed one" or "messiah."

At this point, someone might ask, "Where did this woman get such expensive perfume?" and someone else might (incorrectly) answer, "Wasn't she a prostitute? She obtained the perfume with money that she earned from her immoral profession." Others might be tempted to think of this woman as a sinner who is begging for forgiveness. In the history of biblical interpretation, as early as the sixth century CE, the stories of several women—this Mary (the sister of Martha of Bethany), an unnamed woman who anoints Jesus in Luke 7:36-50, and Mary Magdalene—get collapsed into one story. But in fact, the Gospels present these women as separate characters, and only the unnamed woman in Luke 7:36-50 is identified as "a sinner."

In the first-century Jewish world, a sinner was someone who "missed the mark" by not meeting the expectations of their communitarian culture. Thus, we should not think of Mary of Bethany as a sinner. She is not presented as marginalized from society or in need of restoration to the community. Instead, this story about Mary's anointing of Jesus says a great deal about the nature of true discipleship. First, in response to Judas's complaint about the wastefulness of Mary's action, Jesus

says that Mary should be allowed to keep the perfume for the preparation of his body for burial (John 12:7). Jesus knows that Judas is not concerned about the poor but only about lining his pockets. Remember, too, that the religious authorities have already initiated a plan to kill Jesus (11:45-53). Jesus' words are a reminder that his death is near, and they indicate that Jesus trusts that Mary has already done what is necessary for his burial as he enters into this dark time.

Moreover, in the next chapter of John's Gospel, when Jesus and his disciples enter Jerusalem and gather for a meal, Jesus sets about washing the disciples' feet. Peter protests because his cultural worldview tells him that this task is one that the teacher should not perform (13:6). Jesus tells Peter that he can have no portion or place with him if he does not allow Jesus to wash his feet (13:7-8). What a profound teaching moment for Peter and the other disciples! But Jesus does not explain the message he wants to convey until after he has completed the hospitality ritual: "I have given you a model to follow, so that as I have done for you, you should also do. Amen, amen, I say to you, no slave is greater than his master nor any messenger greater than the one who sent him. If you understand this, blessed are you if you do it" (13:15-17).

Take a moment to let these words sink in. Surely Peter can be excused for not understanding from the start what Jesus was teaching him about discipleship since Jesus' actions, typically performed by a servant or slave, were entirely outside of the cultural norms of his time. However, note that in the chronology of this Gospel, Mary understood the truth of Jesus' message and acted on it even without the benefit of his explicit teaching about service and hospitality. Her bold and loving act of washing Jesus' feet established her as the kind of servant disciple that Jesus wanted all of his disciples to be.

What kind of disciple will you be?

Marys in the New Testament

Name	Description	Main Reference
Mary, the mother of Jesus	Featured in all the Gospels and mentioned in Acts. John alone never names her but calls her "the mother of Jesus."	Matt 1–2; Mark 3:31-35; 6:3; Luke 1–2; John 2:1-12; 19:25-27; Acts 1:14
Mary Magdalene	Recipient of Jesus' healing power. Identified as the first to encounter the risen Lord after the resurrection. Often mistakenly identified with anonymous women who anoint Jesus (Mark 14:3-9; Luke 7:36-50) or with the anonymous woman caught in adultery (John 8:1-11).	Matt 27:56, 61; 28:1; Mark 15:40, 47; 16:1, 9-11; Luke 8:2; 24:10; John 19:25; 20:1, 11-18
Mary of Bethany	Described in Luke as the one who sits at Jesus' feet to listen to him. In John, she is the sister of Lazarus and Martha, and the one who anoints Jesus' feet.	Luke 10:38-42; John 11:1-44; 12:1-8
Mary, mother of James and Joseph (Joses)	One of those who witnesses the crucifixion and burial of Jesus and goes to the empty tomb.	Matt 27:56, 61; 28:1; Mark 15:40, 47; 16:1; Luke 24:10
Mary, wife of Clopas	Witness to the crucifixion along with other faithful women.	John 19:25
Mary, mother of John Mark	Associated with the Jerusalem church.	Acts 12:12
Mary of Rome	Worker in the church at Rome.	Rom 16:6

EXPLORING LESSON FOUR

1. Luke's story of Mary and Martha's encounter with Jesus at Martha's home introduces the theme of hospitality (Luke 10:38-42). Most cultures have rituals around welcoming people into their homes. What practices of hospitality do you or your family have? When you visit someone who has a distinct practice of hospitality, how does it make you feel?

_____

_____

_____

_____

_____

_____

_____

2. As noted above, early manuscripts (handwritten copies) of Luke 10:38-42 allow for two different interpretations of Jesus' response to Martha's complaint. We do not have sufficient evidence to say definitively that one reading is right and the other wrong. Therefore, we are free to entertain both interpretations. Which is most appealing to you and why?

_____

_____

_____

_____

_____

_____

3. Prayerfully reflect on Luke's story of Martha and Mary's encounter with Jesus. With whom do you most identify? As you allow yourself to enter into the story, listen for what Jesus has to say to you. How will you respond?

_____

_____

_____

_____

_____

_____

_____

4. In John's story of the raising of Lazarus (John 11:1-53), we hear almost immediately of Martha and Mary, the sisters of Lazarus, though we do not know for certain that these are the same Martha and Mary of Luke's Gospel (Luke 10:38-42). Compare and contrast the portraits of Martha and Mary in these two Gospels. What do you discover?

_____

_____

_____

_____

_____

5. The story of the raising of Lazarus notes that Jesus waits two days after learning his friend is very ill before beginning his journey to Bethany (John 11:6). Why do you think the Gospel writer included this detail? How does it relate to the message of the story?

_____

_____

_____

_____

_____

6. Carefully examine John 11:7-16, where Jesus tells the disciples about Lazarus's death. Can you find an example of the Johannine literary pattern of double meaning / misunderstanding / clarification? Can you also find examples of Johannine dualism and irony? How do these literary features color your understanding of what Jesus' disciples were like?

_____

_____

_____

_____

_____

7. What is your reaction to the intensity of Jesus' weeping and being "perturbed" toward the end of the story of the raising of Lazarus (John 11:33, 35, 38)? What does it reveal about Jesus' relationship with Mary and Martha?

_____

_____

_____

_____

_____

8. John's story of the raising of Lazarus does not tell us how Martha or Mary reacted to the raising of their brother. However, Jesus asks a question of Martha: "Did I not tell you that if you believe you will see the glory of God?" (John 11:40). Prayerfully reflect on this story. How do you think Martha would have responded? How would you respond today?

_____

_____

_____

_____

_____

9. In John's story of the anointing of Jesus (John 12:1-11), Mary, the sister of Lazarus, is described as performing a ritual of hospitality for Jesus. Her actions would have been considered strange, controversial, and extreme. Have you ever witnessed an act of love or hospitality that was considered extreme and shocking at the time? What do you think prompted this radical act, and how did you and others respond?

_____

_____

_____

_____

_____

10. In John 12:1-11, Mary is presented as a model of discipleship and service even before Jesus teaches his disciples about foot-washing and what true greatness means (John 13:12-17). What does the story about Mary washing Jesus' feet suggest about the nature or attributes of true discipleship and service?

_____

_____

_____

_____

_____

CLOSING PRAYER

Prayer

Mary took a liter of costly perfumed oil made from genuine aromatic nard and anointed the feet of Jesus and dried them with her hair; the house was filled with the fragrance of the oil. (John 12:3)

Gracious and loving God, we thank you for the witness of Mary and Martha, whom the Gospels of Luke and John portray as models of selfless service and radical discipleship. Inspire us and give us the courage to take on your ministries of hospitality with great generosity and to embrace your call to discipleship without fear or shame. This is not for our glory but for yours alone. Inspired by these faithful sisters, we pray today especially for . . .

LESSON FIVE

Mary Magdalene,
Apostle of the Resurrection

Begin your personal study and group discussion with a simple and sincere prayer such as:

Prayer

God of love and consolation, as we study the women of the New Testament, open our hearts and minds to appreciate the unique gifts they each brought to their faith communities. May their witness inspire us today to use the gifts we have received in service of your holy ones.

Read pages 82–93, Lesson Five, highlighting what stands out to you.

Respond to the questions on pages 94–96, Exploring Lesson Five.

The Closing Prayer on page 96 is for your personal use and may be used at the end of group discussion.

MARY MAGDALENE, APOSTLE OF THE RESURRECTION

Mary Magdalene (or Mary of Magdala) appears in all of the passion and resurrection stories of the canonical Gospels, but in some respects, she remains shrouded in mystery and confusion. As early as the second century CE, Christian writers began to conflate the stories about Mary of Magdala with the stories of Mary, the sister of Martha, and with stories about other women in the Gospels, including the unnamed woman whom Luke identifies as "a sinner" (7:36-50). Through this conflation and misidentification, it became common to characterize Mary Magdalene as a prostitute who had repented of her many vices out of love for Jesus.

The most concise of these statements can be found in a homily delivered by Pope Gregory the Great around the year 591 CE:

> The one that Luke calls a sinner [Luke 7:39], and that John names Mary (see John 11:2), we believe that she is that Mary of whom, according to Mark, the Lord has cast out seven demons (cf. Mark 16:9). And what are these seven demons, if not the universality of all vices? Since seven days suffice to embrace the whole of time, the number seven rightly represents universality. Mary had seven demons in her, for she was full of all vices. But now, having seen the stains that dishonored her, she ran to wash herself at the source of mercy, without blushing in the presence of the guests. So great was her shame inside that she could not see anything outside to blush. (*Homilies on the Gospels*, 33)

Modern writers, from novelists to musicians and artists (some drawing upon second-century esoteric writings that were later declared to be heresy), have suggested a rather different but still unhelpful proposition that Mary Magdalene was Jesus' wife and that they even had children together. Our objective in this lesson is to dig deeply into what *the Gospels actually tell us* about Mary Magdalene so that she can shine in her own right as an apostle of the resurrection.

Mary Magdalene in Luke 8:1-3

If we follow the chronology of the Synoptic Gospels, the first mention of Mary Magdalene appears in Luke 8:1-3, where she is named on a list of female followers of Jesus.

> *Luke 8:1-3*
>
> **Galilean Women Follow Jesus.** [1]Afterward [Jesus] journeyed from one town and village to another, preaching and proclaiming the good news of the kingdom of God. Accompanying him were the Twelve [2]and some women who had been cured of evil spirits and infirmities, Mary, called Magdalene, from whom seven demons had gone out, [3]Joanna, the wife of Herod's steward Chuza, Susanna, and many others who provided for them out of their resources.

The opening phrase of this passage can be translated literally as "And it happened that soon afterward." Immediately preceding this passage is the story of the "sinful woman" who washes Jesus' feet with her tears and dries them with her hair (Luke 7:36-50). Is the close literary proximity of these two stories part of the reason that Pope Gregory the Great collapsed them into one narrative? Perhaps, but the biblical text itself does not support that conclusion.

Although we have become accustomed to thinking of "Magdalene" as a synonym for a woman of ill repute, the biblical text suggests no such thing. The attribution "Magdalene" means "a woman of Magdala." The city of Magdala (*Migdal* in Hebrew) was relatively large and prosperous, located on the western shore of the Sea of Galilee, south of Capernaum and north of Tiberias. It was known for preparing and exporting dried fish and for boat building. The city also conducted a robust trade with other parts of the Roman Empire. In this location, archaeologists have discovered a first-century synagogue and ritual baths that drew water from the Sea of Galilee. It is said that St. Helena, the mother of Emperor Constantine, visited the ruins of the city in the fourth century CE and had a basilica built over the site that the locals said was the home of Mary Magdalene. (To date, archaeological evidence of this basilica has not been found, but only approximately 10 percent of the ancient city has been excavated, so more discoveries are certainly possible.)

Magdala is located in the region of Galilee, just west of the Sea of Galilee.

 The Unnamed "Woman Who Was a Sinner"

In the story of the unnamed sinful woman in Luke 7:36-50, we are not told why this woman is considered to be a sinner, but of course, that is not the point of the story. So great is this woman's love for Jesus that this dishonored woman further dishonors herself by breaking into a stranger's dining hall, maneuvering herself to where Jesus (who is the guest of honor) is reclining at table, and weeping so much that she can wash his feet with her tears. The other guests at the table would have been even more shocked to see her taking down her hair and kissing Jesus' feet. This woman gave away whatever honor she had to express her love for Jesus.

In this passage, Luke tells us that Jesus was moving about in Galilee "preaching . . . the good news of the kingdom of God" and that he was accompanied by (literally, "with") the twelve apostles and certain women who had been cured or healed of spirits that were bad (i.e., full of annoyances, hardships, or perils) and infirmities or feebleness of health (8:1-2). At that time, illnesses and deviant behavior that was outside of a person's control were thought to be caused by evil spirits.

Also note that possession by evil spirits was not associated with an individual's moral wrongdoing. From this description, we can conclude only that Mary of Magdala was very, very sick at the time she first encountered Jesus' healing presence. (The number seven, representing the number of "demons" that Jesus expelled from Mary Magdalene [8:2], is a perfect number or a number representing fullness. In other words, Mary was as sick as anyone could be without dying before Jesus healed her.)

What more can we say about this woman who is identified as Mary Magdalene (meaning "of the town of Magdala")? Males living in the first century CE were usually identified with the city of their origin or their current location. (Surnames did not come into use until the beginning of the eleventh century CE.) Women, by contrast, were usually identified in relation to the male who was their guardian (e.g., "Joanna, the wife of Herod's steward Chuza"; 8:3). That Mary was known as "Mary Magdalene" (or "Mary of Magdala" in John's Gospel) might indicate that she was widowed or divorced—perhaps her husband abandoned her when she was ill—or that she was independently a person of high social standing in the city of Magdala.

The phrase translated in Luke 8:3 as "out of their resources" can be translated as "out of their own means" or "out of what belonged to them," which suggests that these women had financial independence apart from their husbands' or families' resources. Three of these women had high enough social standing to be remembered by their own names. In other

words, these women were not on the margins of society as one might expect of a prostitute. Instead, we can reasonably conclude that Mary of Magdala and the rest of these women who were healed by Jesus were well-respected and financially independent women who supported Jesus and the Twelve as a form of reciprocity for his kindness toward them.

Mary Magdalene in the Passion and Resurrection Narratives of the Synoptic Gospels

If we continue to follow the chronology of the Synoptic Gospels, the next mention of Mary Magdalene is as one of the witnesses to Jesus' crucifixion:

Mark 15:40-41

[40]There were also women looking on from a distance. Among them were Mary Magdalene, Mary the mother of the younger James and of Joses, and Salome. [41]These women had followed him when he was in Galilee and ministered to him. There were also many other women who had come up with him to Jerusalem.

Matthew 27:55-56

[5]There were many women there, looking on from a distance, who had followed Jesus from Galilee, ministering to him. [56]Among them were Mary Magdalene and Mary the mother of James and Joseph, and the mother of the sons of Zebedee.

Luke 23:48-49

[48]When all the people who had gathered for this spectacle saw what had happened, they returned home beating their breasts; [49]but all his acquaintances stood at a distance, including the women who had followed him from Galilee and saw these events.

Luke's Gospel groups the female witnesses of Jesus' crucifixion together with the attribution "the women who had followed him from Galilee" (23:49), but we can safely assume that Mary Magdalene is included in this group because of her inclusion in Luke 8:1-3 (which describes a group of women who traveled with Jesus from Galilee). The fact that she is listed first in both Mark and Matthew suggests her prominence among the female followers of Jesus from Galilee.

Next, we turn to the post-resurrection narratives in the Synoptic Gospels. Again, Mary Magdalene is mentioned first among the witnesses to the empty tomb in the Gospels of Mark and Matthew:

Mark 16:1

¹When the sabbath was over, Mary Magdalene, Mary, the mother of James, and Salome bought spices so that they might go and anoint him.

Matthew 28:1

¹After the sabbath, as the first day of the week was dawning, Mary Magdalene and the other Mary came to see the tomb.

A second ending to Mark's Gospel, added by a later scribe, names Mary Magdalene as the first to see the risen Christ. Note the reference to "seven demons," a phrase first associated with Mary Magdalene in Luke 8:1-3:

Mark 16:9-11

⁹When he had risen, early on the first day of the week, he appeared first to Mary Magdalene, out of whom he had driven seven demons. ¹⁰She went and told his companions who were mourning and weeping. ¹¹When they heard that he was alive and had been seen by her, they did not believe.

 Various Endings of Mark's Gospel

The Gospel of Mark, which most biblical scholars believe to be the earliest of the New Testament Gospels, has several endings. The original ending of Mark (16:1-8) is strange and surprising because there are no appearances of the risen Christ, and because the Gospel concludes with the statement that the witnesses of the empty tomb "went out and fled from the tomb, seized with trembling and bewilderment. They said nothing to anyone, for they were afraid" (16:8). How can we call Mark's Gospel "good news" when the witnesses of the resurrection run away and tell no one?

What is now called the "Longer Ending" (16:9-20) seems to have been added in the late second century CE, perhaps in response to the question above. What is now called the "Shorter Ending" was probably added in the fourth century and is now placed between 16:8 and 16:9.

A good study Bible will mark these two additions with square brackets, headings, or footnotes, so you know that they were not part of the original ending of Mark's Gospel. However, at the Council of Trent (1545–63), it was decided that the Gospel of Mark should include these verses. Thus the "Longer Ending" of Mark's Gospel (16:9-20) is considered canonical biblical material.

The fourth-century "Freer Logion," named after the man who discovered the manuscript in 1906 and now housed at the Smithsonian's Freer Gallery of Art, may also be included in the footnotes of your study Bible. It is an additional saying of Jesus (a "logion") that was inserted in that manuscript after Mark 16:14.

The author of Luke's Gospel uses the attribution "[t]he women who had come from Galilee with him" to identify the first witnesses to the empty tomb, but remember that Mary Magdalene is included in this group (see Luke 8:1-3, where she is listed first):

Luke 23:55–24:3

[55]The women who had come from Galilee with him followed behind, and when they had seen the tomb and the way in which his body was laid in it, [56]they returned and prepared spices and perfumed oils. Then they rested on the sabbath according to the commandment.

The Resurrection of Jesus. [1]But at daybreak on the first day of the week they took the spices they had prepared and went to the tomb. [2]They found the stone rolled away from the tomb; [3]but when they entered, they did not find the body of the Lord Jesus.

Finally, the Synoptic Gospels provide two brief mentions of Mary Magdalene, accompanied by other women, encountering the resurrected Jesus (in Matthew) or "two men in dazzling garments" (in Luke) and being given the task of telling the disciples what she has seen:

Matthew 28:8-10

[8]Then they [Mary Magdalene and the other Mary] went away quickly from the tomb, fearful yet overjoyed, and ran to announce this to his disciples. [9]And behold, Jesus met them on their way and greeted them. They approached, embraced his feet, and did him homage. [10]Then Jesus said to them, "Do not be afraid. Go tell my brothers to go to Galilee, and there they will see me."

Luke 24:4-11

[4]While they [the women who had come from Galilee] were puzzling over this [the empty tomb], behold, two men in dazzling garments appeared to them. [5]They were terrified and bowed their faces to the ground. They said to them, "Why do you seek the living one among the dead? [6]He is not here, but he has been raised. Remember what he said to you while he was still in Galilee, [7]that the Son of Man must be handed over to sinners and be crucified, and rise on the third day." [8]And they remembered his words. [9]Then they returned from the tomb and announced all these things to the eleven and to all the others. [10]The women were Mary Magdalene, Joanna, and Mary the mother of James; the others who accompanied them also told this to the apostles, [11]but their story seemed like nonsense and they did not believe them.

Mary Magdalene and the women at the tomb. The Latin phrase Surrexit Non Est Hic *means "He is not here" (Matt 28:6).*

Whether or not the disciples believe them, these women are the first witnesses and evangelizers of Jesus' resurrection. Glory, alleluia!

Mary Magdalene in the Gospel of John

The portrait of Mary Magdalene in the Gospel of John is quite different. She appears only briefly at Jesus' crucifixion, but later, in a somewhat lengthy scene, she is described as the first witness and apostle of his resurrection. First, let us examine what is said of her as a witness of Jesus' crucifixion:

John 19:25-27

[25]Standing by the cross of Jesus were his mother and his mother's sister, Mary the wife of Clopas, and Mary of Magdala. [26]When Jesus saw his mother and the disciple there whom he loved, he said to his mother, "Woman, behold, your son." [27]Then he said to the disciple, "Behold, your mother." And from that hour the disciple took her into his home.

Notice that in this verse, Mary of Magdala is mentioned last among the female witnesses to Jesus' crucifixion. Only Mary of Magdala is described in terms of her place name, suggesting she has no attachment to family. Nothing is said about her past illness or her moral character. That these women are standing by the cross speaks to their courage in facing suffering even to the point of death. Women in this setting would have been the recipients of significant abuse from the crowds who were present for the spectacle of death on a cross. Note that of Jesus' male disciples, only the Beloved Disciple is mentioned as being present to witness his death.

John's story of the empty tomb and the appearance of the resurrected Christ is quite elaborate by comparison to the accounts in the Synoptic Gospels. The narrative is organized as an intercalation, a story within a story, but in

John 20:1-18

[1]On the first day of the week, Mary of Magdala came to the tomb early in the morning, while it was still dark, and saw the stone removed from the tomb.

Intercalated story begins here:

[2]So she ran and went to Simon Peter and to the other disciple whom Jesus loved, and told them, "They have taken the Lord from the tomb, and we don't know where they put him." [3]So Peter and the other disciple went out and came to the tomb. [4]They both ran, but the other disciple ran faster than Peter and arrived at the tomb first; [5]he bent down and saw the burial cloths there, but did not go in. [6]When Simon Peter arrived after him, he went into the tomb and saw the burial cloths there, [7]and the cloth that had covered his head, not with the burial cloths but rolled up in a separate place. [8]Then the other disciple also went in, the one who had arrived at the tomb first, and he saw and believed. [9]For they did not yet understand the scripture that he had to rise from the dead. [10]Then the disciples returned home.

End of intercalated story.

[11]But Mary stayed outside the tomb weeping. And as she wept, she bent over into the tomb [12]and saw two angels in white sitting there, one at the head and one at the feet where the body of Jesus had been. [13]And they said to her, "Woman, why are you weeping?" She said to them, "They have taken my Lord, and I don't know where they laid him." [14]When she had said this, she turned around and saw Jesus there, but did not know it was Jesus. [15]Jesus said to her, "Woman, why are you weeping? Whom are you looking for?" She thought it was the gardener and said to him, "Sir, if you carried him away, tell me where you laid him, and I will take him." [16]Jesus said to her, "Mary!" She turned and said to him in Hebrew, "Rabbouni," which means Teacher. [17]Jesus said to her, "Stop holding on to me, for I have not yet ascended to the Father. But go to my brothers and tell them, 'I am going to my Father and your Father, to my God and your God.'" [18]Mary of Magdala went and announced to the disciples, "I have seen the Lord," and what he told her.

this case, the outer story is of greater importance in moving the plot forward and in carrying the message of belief for the Christian community.

The story begins with a description of the setting. It is "the first day of the week" (20:1). Since the Sabbath is on the seventh day of the week, this is a Sunday. It is very early in the morning, before dawn. Night was generally considered to be a dangerous time when dark spirits were most active and most powerful. But darkness and light are also dualistic opposites in this Gospel, symbolizing unbelief and belief. Mary Magdalene is portrayed as miserable and even somewhat crazed over the loss of her teacher. Could the narrator be telling us that she is still "in the dark," metaphorically speaking, but that soon the light of dawn will come upon her?

Moving to the intercalated story, the narrator describes Mary Magdalene running to tell Peter and the Beloved Disciple that Jesus' tomb is empty. She greets them with the first of three laments: "They have taken the Lord from the tomb, and we don't know where they put him" (20:2). Peter and the Beloved Disciple arrive at the tomb, and after seeing the burial cloths arranged in such a way as to suggest that this was not a "snatch and grab" grave robbery, they "go back to their own [place or stuff]" (20:10, my translation). Although translations often insert "homes" into this verse, the point is clear: Peter and the Beloved Disciple are more "in the dark" than is Mary Magdalene because, having witnessed the empty tomb, they simply go back to where they came from. Even the Beloved Disciple's initial faith ("he saw and believed"; 20:8) is not enough to keep him there. What a disappointment! The narrator explains their failure to understand what they had seen: "For they did not yet understand the scripture that he had to rise from the dead" (20:9). The disciples remain "in the dark" both literally and figuratively until John 20:18, when Mary goes to their hiding place (see 20:19) to deliver the message of the resurrection.

Returning now to the outer story of this intercalation, we find Mary weeping outside of the tomb. Let us consider this scene and what it may tell us about Mary Magdalene. In the burial scene of John's Gospel, the narrator describes the place where Jesus' body was laid to rest as "a garden" (19:41). As Mary Magdalene weeps, she peers, or "ben[ds] over" (Greek *parakuptó*, meaning "to stoop and look" or "to look intensely"), into the tomb (20:11). Seeing Mary of Magdala as a distraught woman running around alone at night and in great danger from human predators has prompted some interpreters of this post-resurrection story to compare her story to the allegory of the bride and bridegroom in the Song of Songs. The bride represents Israel, and the bridegroom is God. In Song of Songs 3:1-5 and 5:2-8, we learn of the woman's search for her lover, who came knocking at her door during the night and then disappeared. She goes out into the city and along the streets, looking for her lover, and is even beaten by the night watchmen as she laments her loss. While we cannot say with any certainty that the Gospel writer intended to evoke the beautiful and profound poetry of the Song of Songs, it gives us a sense of the intensity of Mary's grief over the loss of her teacher. She loved Jesus with a great love—the love of Israel for God!

When Mary looks through her tears into the tomb, she sees an amazing sight. Two angel messengers are seated at the head and foot of the stone slab where Jesus' body would have been laid (John 20:12). When they ask why she is weeping, all she can muster is another lament: "They have taken my Lord, and I don't know where they laid him" (20:13). As it is used here, the title "Lord" means "Sir" or "Master." Mary does not yet recognize Jesus' true identity. She understands only that Jesus is dead and that someone has taken his body.

Mary then hears another voice asking her the same question, and for a third time, she laments: "Sir, if you carried him away, tell me where you laid him, and I will take him." There are two important things to notice in the response she receives. First, the risen Jesus says to her, "Whom are you looking for?" (20:15). This is essentially the same question Jesus asked when he met his first followers and extended the invitation "Come . . . and see," a call to discipleship (John 1:38-39). Is Jesus' question to Mary a renewed invitation to discipleship? Second, notice that it is not until Jesus calls her by name, *Mariam*, that she recognizes him. She responds, "Rabbouni," which the Gospel writer clarifies as meaning "Teacher!" or "Teacher?" (20:16; it is not clear whether her response is exclamatory or questioning, because the early Greek manuscripts do not include punctuation). Note that *rabbouni*, a Greek transliteration of an Aramaic or Hebrew word, literally means "*my* teacher." How significant is it that Mary Magdalene calls Jesus "*my* teacher" rather than simply using the term *rabbi* ("teacher")?

In addition to the use of the Greek word **parakuptó** to describe Mary Magdalene peering into the tomb where Jesus was buried (John 20:11), it is used of the Beloved Disciple in John 20:5 and of Peter in Luke 24:12. It is also used in James 1:25 and 1 Peter 1:12 in the sense of looking intently into spiritual realities.

Jesus' response to Mary—which the NABRE translates as "Stop holding on to me, for I have not yet ascended to the Father. But go to my brothers and tell them, 'I am going to my Father and your Father, to my God and your God'" (20:17)—has prompted considerable debate among modern biblical scholars. Some have argued that this detail is a variant of what we see in Matthew's Gospel, where the risen Christ appears to Mary Magdalene and the other Mary, and they take hold of his feet and worship him (Matt 28:9). Others argue that there is something unusual about Jesus' pre-ascension resurrected body that makes it inappropriate for her to touch him. But later, when the risen Jesus appears to the disciples, he invites Thomas to touch the wounds in his hands, feet, and side (John 20:27). Still others say that Jesus' words to Mary signal that the risen Christ will not be controlled or held against his will. Another perhaps more intriguing option involves making one change to the punctuation of the NABRE translation. Remember that early Greek

The garden tomb in Jerusalem, venerated by Christians as the burial site of Jesus according to John's Gospel (19:41-42).

manuscripts did not include punctuation. Thus, the statement could read like this: "Do not cling to me. Since I have not yet ascended to the Father, go to my brothers and tell them" (my translation).

Either way, Mary Magdalene is sent by the risen Christ on a mission to proclaim the resurrection to Jesus' other disciples. The word *apostle* means "one who is sent." Although the perception of Mary Magdalene as a reformed prostitute persists in Western Christianity, among Eastern Orthodox Christians, she is consistently known as the apostle of the resurrection. In a legend dating back to at least the sixth century CE, it was said that Mary of Magdala went to Rome to visit Emperor Tiberius, carrying a white egg to preach about Jesus' resurrection. Tiberius responded scornfully, saying that God could no more raise the dead than he could turn her white egg red. Instantly, the egg turned red! Thus, Eastern Orthodox icons of Mary Magdalene often show her holding either a white or red egg in celebration of that miracle.

 The first reading for the **feast of Saint Mary Magdalene** (July 22) is Song of Songs 3:1-4b, which includes the words, "I sought him but I did not find him. . . . Have you seen him whom my heart loves?" The psalm response is: "My soul is thirsting for you, O Lord my God" (Ps 63:2), and the Gospel reading is John 20:1-2, 11-18.

John's account of Mary Magdalene encountering the risen Jesus ends with Mary Magdalene going to Jesus' disciples, who had hidden themselves away in fear of the religious authorities who had instigated Jesus' crucifixion. She boldly proclaims the good news: "I have seen the Lord" (20:18). Here we are presented with two very different options for our own response to Jesus' resurrection. Will we go into hiding like the disciples, out of fear of what others might do to us, or will we be like Mary of Magdala, who clearly and fearlessly declares her faith in the living Christ?

How Mary Magdalene Became a (Repentant) Prostitute

The homilies of Pope Gregory the Great (c. 591 CE) provide our first written evidence that several Gospel stories (the story of the "sinful woman" who washes Jesus' feet with her tears in Luke 7:36-50; the story of Mary, the sister of Lazarus, anointing Jesus in John 12:1-11; and the stories of Mary Magdalene, the first witness of the resurrection) were being conflated into a single story about a repentant prostitute who encountered the resurrected Christ and was told to deliver a message to the apostles. However, it is possible that this conflation began as early as the second century CE, when early Christians began to create Gospel harmonies in an effort to construct a single story of Jesus' life, death, and resurrection from the four canonical Gospels in order to resolve some of the inconsistencies among them.

Jane Schaberg, author of *The Resurrection of Mary Magdalene*, offers a list of seven Gospel stories and notes the commonalities that may have contributed to the conflation of the sinful woman, Mary the sister of Lazarus, and Mary Magdalene. Here is her list, which does not include the Gospel stories explicitly associated with Mary Magdalene:

1. An unnamed woman anoints Jesus' head as a prophetic gesture related to his death (Mark 14:3-9; Matt 26:6-13).
2. Mary, the sister of Lazarus, anoints Jesus' feet with perfume as a prophetic gesture related to his death (John 12:1-8).
3. An unnamed female "sinner" enters the home of Simon the Pharisee and washes Jesus' feet with her tears, wipes them with her hair, kisses them, and anoints them with ointment (Luke 7:36-50).
4. Mary sits at Jesus' feet while Martha waits on him (Luke 10:38-42).

5. An unnamed woman is caught in adultery (John 7:53–8:11).
6. The Samaritan woman (who is often assumed to be a prostitute, though the text does not state this to be the case) talks with Jesus (John 4:4-42).
7. The unnamed bride at the wedding feast of Cana is a recipient of Jesus' first sign (John 2:1-11).

One obvious connection that is shared among many of these stories is the theme of anointing, though the story of the female "sinner" who washes Jesus' feet with her tears does not include the prophetic element of preparation for burial. Several of these stories have also been interpreted to allude to a woman having committed a sexual sin of some sort. All but the story of the woman caught in adultery and the story of the wedding feast at Cana assume some level of intimacy between Jesus and a woman. We can add to these similarities the fact that the name Mary appears frequently in the Gospels and in other Jewish literature of the time. Schaberg notes that early church writers who were trying to harmonize or clear up discrepancies among the Gospels could easily confuse one with the other.

However, both Schaberg and Susan Haskins, author of *Mary Magdalen: Myth and Metaphor*, suggest that something more sinister, whether conscious or unconscious, might have been at work in the remaking of Mary Magdalene's image over time. Luke's reference to Mary Magdalene having been possessed by seven demons (Luke 8:2) was particularly problematic. In the ancient Mediterranean world, women were thought to be more vulnerable to demon possession because they were considered to be the weaker sex. Since the number seven symbolized totality or fullness, and because women were considered dangerous from a sexual point of view, it was easy for people to conclude that Mary Magdalene's demon possession involved sexual sin. But Pope Gregory the Great went even further and interpreted the seven evil spirits that were driven out of Mary Magdalene as the sum total of the seven deadly sins, which are traditionally known as pride, greed, lust, envy, gluttony, wrath, and sloth (*Homilies on the Gospels*, 33).

Earlier religious texts like Sirach 26:10-12 and 1 Timothy 2:11-15, with their cautionary warnings about unruly women, easily set the scene for such escalation of negative attitudes toward women:

The Magdalene Laundries

A much darker legacy of the conflation of the biblical Mary Magdalene stories with the stories of Mary of Bethany and the unnamed "sinner" who washes Jesus' feet with her tears in Luke 7:36-50 can be found in Ireland's "Magdalene laundries," also called mother-and-baby homes. These laundries were set up as places for unwed mothers and prostitutes, with the stated mission of penitence and reform. In reality, they were places of hard labor and lifetime incarceration for women and girls who did not conform to what was considered socially acceptable behavior for women.

Although much of the documentation related to the Magdalene laundries has been kept secret, some estimate that 30,000 women and girls were housed in these church-run institutions during the eighteenth through twentieth centuries. The last one was closed in 1996 and was slated for demolition but will instead be preserved as a public memorial and education center to tell the stories of those who suffered abuse and detention under this system that was given credibility under the moniker of Mary Magdalene, the "repentant sinner."

Keep a strict watch over an unruly wife,
  lest, finding an opportunity, she use it;
[11] Watch out for her impudent eye,
  and do not be surprised if she betrays you:
[12] As a thirsty traveler opens his mouth
  and drinks from any water nearby,
So she sits down before every tent peg
  and opens her quiver for every arrow.
  (Sir 26:10-12)

A woman must receive instruction silently and under complete control. [12] I do not permit a woman to teach or to have authority over a man. She must be quiet. [13] For Adam was formed first, then Eve. [14] Further, Adam was not deceived, but the woman was deceived and transgressed. [15] But she will be saved through motherhood, provided women persevere in faith and love and holiness, with self-control. (1 Tim 2:11-15)

Tertullian (c. 160–225 CE) drew upon similar imagery of women patterned after the deceived Eve, but in even harsher terms:

And do you not know that you are (each) an Eve? The sentence of God on this sex of yours lives in this age: the guilt of necessity must live too. *You* are the devil's gateway: *you* are the unsealer of that (forbidden) tree: *you* are the first deserter of the divine law: *you* are she who persuaded him whom the devil was not valiant enough to attack. *You* destroyed so easily God's image, man. (*On the Apparel of Women* I.1)

On a somewhat more positive note, though still problematic, Ambrose of Milan (c. 339–97 CE) wrote that it was appropriate for Mary Magdalene to be the one who first witnessed Christ's resurrection:

For Mary worshipped Christ, and therefore is appointed to be the messenger of the Resurrection to the apostles, loosening the hereditary bond, and the huge offense of womankind. . . . And rightly is a woman appointed [as messenger] to men; that she who first had brought the message of sin to man should first bring the message of the grace of the Lord. (*On the Holy Spirit* III.11.74)

At the risk of oversimplifying a very complex and conflictual history of interpretation of the now conflated traditions assigned to Mary Magdalene, there arose over time a number of legends about her that had little to do with the biblical stories. Mary Magdalene's role as the first witness to Jesus' resurrection and the one sent to preach the good news to the apostles slowly became drained of its power by characterizations of her as a repentant prostitute, the stain of whose sin could not be fully erased.

By conflating Luke's reference to the seven demons that were driven out of her (Luke 8:2) with the story of the anonymous female who washes Jesus' feet with her tears and dries them with her hair (Luke 7:36-50), Mary Magdalene gained greater notoriety as the "madwoman in Christianity's attic," to borrow the words of Jane Schaberg, than as the "apostle to the apostles." After all, who doesn't love a tantalizing story?

Legends about Mary Magdalene grew in popularity and appeal from the tenth through the twelfth centuries. One such legend suggests that Mary was the unnamed bride in the story of the wedding feast at Cana (John 2:1-11). According to this legend, the apostle John was her intended bridegroom, but he abandoned her to follow Jesus. Her response was to flee Cana, become a prostitute, and set up a brothel in Jerusalem, which became a temple of demons. Thus, the story explains how Mary Magdalene took on a life of prostitution and how she came to be possessed by seven demons.

Another legend describes the extent of Mary Magdalene's penitence for her former life of sin, perhaps even borrowing details from the story of Mary of Egypt, a prostitute turned penitent saint who is greatly honored in the Eastern and Coptic Churches as one of the Desert Mothers and who also has a feast day in the Catholic tradition. Mary of Egypt is said to have lived in the desert for so long that she was naked because her clothes had disintegrated and that she was then covered only by her long hair. Some legends about Mary Magdalene describe her as living in the desert for thirty years in repentance for her life as a prostitute, and sometimes she is depicted in art as completely naked, like Mary of Egypt, or only partially covered as a reminder of her past life as a prostitute.

Another of the legends about Mary Magdalene holds that she and some of her colleagues were expelled by the Romans from the Holy Land on a rudderless boat with the intention that they would die at sea, but miraculously, they landed safely in Provence in southeastern France at what would later be called Saintes-Maries-de-la-Mer (translated "Saint Marys of the Sea"), for the three who disembarked from the boat were Mary Jacobe, Mary Salome, and Mary Magdalene. Eventually the group dispersed, and Mary Magdalene went on with Lazarus to convert the people of Marseille before departing to the desert. These legends also attribute many miracles to Mary Magdalene, most of which involve advocacy for parents and children.

This is just a small taste of what is included among the legends of Mary Magdalene. The stories are exciting and entertaining, but they also reflect strong popular devotion to Mary Magdalene by Christians through the medieval period and well into the time of the Reformation in the sixteenth century. In essence, Mary Magdalene became the archetype of the truly repentant sinner whose love for Jesus was so great that she continued to receive divine grace after the demons were expelled from her and she was forgiven of her sins. But very little was said about her role as the post-resurrection apostle to the apostles. Was this omission simply an accident of history, or was it a more deliberate attempt to downplay her extraordinary role in contrast to that of the male disciples of Jesus?

Today, a great majority of biblical scholars recognize that the Gospel stories about Mary Magdalene are separate from those of Mary the sister of Lazarus and the unnamed "sinner" who washed Jesus' feet with her tears. However, once the image of a weeping and repentant Mary Magdalene became firmly embedded in people's minds through medieval religious art and literature, etc., we lost our focus on what the Gospels actually say about her.

In fact, Mary Magdalene was classified as a "penitent" by the Roman Catholic Church until 1969, when the Roman Catholic calendar of saints was revised. More recently, in 2016, with the approval of Pope Francis, the Vatican Congregation for Divine Worship and the Discipline of the Sacraments issued a decree that the liturgical memorial of Mary Magdalene would become a feast "like the rest of the apostles," and that her feast day Mass would have its own preface entitled *"de apostolorum apostola"* ("apostle of the apostles"). Thus, after approximately 1,400 years, Mary Magdalene has been officially released from the shackles of a purported life of sin and has been set free to be who she is: "an example of true and authentic evangelization" (Vatican Bulletin, "Mary Magdalene, Apostle of the Apostles," Oct. 6, 2016).

EXPLORING LESSON FIVE

1. One reason interpreters of the Gospels have labeled Mary Magdalene as a sinner is because of the mention of her having been possessed by demons (Luke 8:1-2). However, if we understand demon possession in its historical and cultural context as an illness that requires healing (rather than an indication of sin), what can we say about Mary Magdalene and her disposition toward Jesus?

_____

_____

_____

_____

_____

2. The Synoptic Gospels present Mary Magdalene as one of the women who witness Jesus' crucifixion and later his empty tomb. Notice, however, that Jesus' disciples are nowhere to be found. Apparently they went into hiding after Jesus' arrest. What attributes or character traits would you associate with these women that make them different from Jesus' disciples?

_____

_____

_____

_____

_____

3. Note one thing you learned from the commentary section on "Mary Magdalene in Luke 8:1-3" that helped you sort out what we actually know about Mary Magdalene from this passage.

_____

_____

_____

_____

4. In John's intercalated story of the empty tomb (John 20:1-18), locate the outer story in which Mary of Magdala comes to Jesus' tomb in the early morning, while it is still dark. Using what you know about the dualism of John's Gospel, what does this small detail tell us about her state of belief at the beginning of the story?

_____

_____

_____

_____

5. In this same story, the narrator tells us that Mary Magdalene cried out three times with some version of the lament, "They have taken away the Lord." How does this detail impact what you think about Mary Magdalene and how she must have felt about Jesus?

---

6. At least a few biblical scholars have observed similarities in tone and even vocabulary between John's story of Mary Magdalene's visit to Jesus' tomb and the story of the bride searching for her bridegroom in the Old Testament book Song of Songs (Songs 3:1-5; 5:2-8). What does this connection add to our portrait of Mary Magdalene? (Note: Song of Songs is an allegory about God as the bridegroom and Israel as the bride. The bride expresses her love for the bridegroom as she searches for him in the night.)

---

7. Returning to John's intercalated story of the empty tomb (John 20:1-18), locate the inner story in which Peter and the other disciple, also known as the Beloved Disciple, come to Jesus' tomb. Why do you think the narrator notes that the other disciple waits to enter the tomb until after Peter arrives? (See also John 21:15-23.) Compare the disciples' response to what they see at the tomb with Mary Magdalene's response.

---

8. According to the commentary, there are several possible manuscript readings of the risen Jesus' words to Mary Magdalene when she attempts to touch him (John 20:17). Which of these readings do you prefer and why?

---

9. Because of John's story of the empty tomb, Mary Magdalene has long been seen by Eastern Christianity, and now more recently by the Roman Catholic tradition, as the "apostle to the apostles." How does this title confirm or expand the way you think about Mary Magdalene? Have any other details from this lesson changed your perception or increased your knowledge about Mary Magdalene?

_____

_____

_____

_____

_____

CLOSING PRAYER

Prayer

Mary of Magdala went and announced to the disciples, "I have seen the Lord" . . .

(John 20:18)

Loving and living God, we thank you for the witness of St. Mary of Magdala, the apostle to the apostles. She and the women who accompanied her supported Jesus and the twelve from their resources. So great was her love for Jesus and her gratitude for her healing that she kept vigil at his dying and returned to his tomb to grieve his death. And so great was your graciousness to her that you allowed her to behold Jesus in his resurrected state. May we, like Mary Magdalene, accept our role as apostles of the resurrection to a sad and troubled world. Inspired by her love and strength, we pray today especially for . . .

LESSON SIX

Other Important But Lesser-Known Women of the New Testament

Begin your personal study and group discussion with a simple and sincere prayer such as:

Prayer

God of love and consolation, as we study the women of the New Testament, open our hearts and minds to appreciate the unique gifts they each brought to their faith communities. May their witness inspire us today to use the gifts we have received in service of your holy ones.

Read pages 98–109, Lesson Six, highlighting what stands out to you.

Respond to the questions on pages 110–112, Exploring Lesson Six.

The Closing Prayer on page 113 is for your personal use and may be used at the end of group discussion.

OTHER IMPORTANT BUT LESSER-KNOWN WOMEN OF THE NEW TESTAMENT

This lesson will focus on some of the lesser-known women, named and unnamed, who appear only briefly in the New Testament. First, we will look at some Gospel parables. Among the few dozen parables in the Synoptic Gospels (John's Gospel has none), only four have women as major characters. Two are found in Luke's Gospel, and two are in Matthew's Gospel. None of the female characters in these parables have names, but this is common for parables. Second, we will examine stories about women who were involved in the ministry of the early church. Their stories come from the Acts of the Apostles and Paul's letters.

Before we can examine the four parables that have women as their major characters, we need to define the literary form so we know what to expect of a parable. Although there are several definitions of a parable, perhaps the clearest and most revealing definition was articulated by New Testament scholar C. H. Dodd. He wrote, "At its simplest the parable is a metaphor or simile drawn from nature or common life, arresting the hearer by its vividness or strangeness, and leaving the mind in sufficient doubt about its precise application to tease it into active thought" (*The Parables of the Kingdom*, 1961).

With C. H. Dodd's definition as a starting point, here are a few additional observations about parables. First, parables are fictional stories about everyday life that are designed to teach a lesson. The Greek word *parabole* means "a comparison" or "a juxtaposition." Sometimes the comparison being made is explicit, as in "The kingdom of God is like . . ." Sometimes the comparison must be discerned from the literary context—what comes before and after it in the biblical text. In fact, the literary context often tells us a great deal about the message of the parable. Finally, Dodd notes that a parable typically has some interesting twist or surprise that makes us think more deeply about its meaning.

The parable of the yeast is a good example of a parable drawn from nature or common life. Everyone in first-century Palestine would have been able to relate to a story about a woman making bread:

Matthew 13:33

The Parable of the Yeast. [33]He spoke to them another parable. "The kingdom of heaven is like yeast that a woman took and mixed with three measures of wheat flour until the whole batch was leavened."

The narrator of this parable tells us that the flour is wheaten flour or meal, which would have been leavened with something like a sourdough starter. When a small amount of leavening is added to "three measures of wheat flour" (13:33; approximately 168 cups in US units of measure) it will make an extremely large amount of bread! The point of the parable is that, although the kingdom of heaven (the leavening) might appear minimal and even somewhat inert at its beginning, it will grow to overflowing. Thus, this woman is presented as an agent of the generative and overflowing reign of God.

Likewise, the parable of the persistent widow is drawn from a scene that would have been recognizable to anyone living in the first-century Mediterranean world:

Luke 18:1-8

The Parable of the Persistent Widow. [1]Then he told them a parable about the necessity for them to pray always without becoming weary. He said, [2]"There was a judge in a certain town who neither feared God nor respected any human being. [3]And a widow in that town used to come to him and say, 'Render a just decision for me against my adversary.' [4]For a long time the judge was unwilling, but eventually he thought, 'While it is true that I neither fear God nor respect any human being, [5]because this widow keeps bothering me I shall deliver a just decision for her lest she finally come and strike me.'" [6]The Lord said, "Pay attention to what the dishonest judge says. [7]Will not God then secure the rights of his chosen ones who call out to him day and night? Will he be slow to answer them? [8]I tell you, he will see to it that justice is done for them speedily. But when the Son of Man comes, will he find faith on earth?"

It was common practice for elders to set themselves up at the gates of a town or village to judge cases that came before them. The message of this parable is that persistence in prayer pays off. If this woman with very few rights in a first-century court can get a judge who "neither fear[ed] God nor respect[ed] any human being" to decide in her favor (18:4-5), how much more will God, who is judge over all the earth and who honors the least among God's chosen ones, respond to the petitions of those who pray "day and night" (18:7)? Thus, this woman is held up as an example of admirable persistence, pointing us toward God's bountiful mercy that is given to those who are persistent in prayer.

The parable of the ten virgins reflects another scene that those living in the first-century Mediterranean world would have known well:

Matthew 25:1-13

The Parable of the Ten Virgins. [1]"Then the kingdom of heaven will be like ten virgins who took their lamps and went out to meet the bridegroom. [2]Five of them were foolish and five were wise. [3]The foolish ones, when taking their lamps, brought no oil with them, [4]but the wise brought flasks of oil with their lamps. [5]Since the bridegroom was long delayed, they all became drowsy and fell asleep. [6]At midnight, there was a cry, 'Behold, the bridegroom! Come out to meet him!' [7]Then all those virgins got up and trimmed their lamps. [8]The foolish ones said to the wise, 'Give us some of your oil, for our lamps are going out.' [9]But the wise ones replied, 'No, for there may not be enough for us and you. Go instead to the merchants and buy some for yourselves.' [10]While they went off to buy it, the bridegroom came and those who were ready went into the wedding feast with him. Then the door was locked. [11]Afterwards the other virgins came and said, 'Lord, Lord, open the door for us!' [12]But he said in reply, 'Amen, I say to you, I do not know you.' [13]Therefore, stay awake, for you know neither the day nor the hour.

In this parable, the Gospel writer is using wedding imagery to remind his early Christian community that the risen Christ, the heavenly bridegroom, could return at any moment, so they should always stay ready like the five wise wedding attendants in the story. If they do not, they could be left out in the cold like the five foolish attendants. The most important part of the wedding festivities was when the bride was transferred from her father's home to her new husband's home, which was often somewhere near or even within his father's home. When the transfer was complete, the bride and groom would consummate their marriage. The attendants (all of whom would have been not-yet-married teenagers) would wait outside until the couple emerged from the bridal chamber. They would then proceed to the wedding feast.

In the first-century Mediterranean world, marriages were contractual relationships between families for the purpose of establishing alliances or protecting family resources, so the **betrothal contract** was an important first step in the process. Fathers would make these betrothal agreements on behalf of their children when they were as young as ten or twelve years old.

According to the parable, only five of the young girls in the wedding party are present when the newly married couple emerges from the bridal chamber. The other five, who were not prepared for the couple's delay, are off doing what they should have done before the wedding ceremonies began. Therefore, they miss their opportunity to accompany the bride and groom into the banquet area for lots of feasting, the banquet being the symbol for the now-arrived reign of God. The five wise virgins remind us that we must be prepared to wait as long as it takes to share in the fullness of God's reign. Indeed, the time will come.

The parable of the lost coin is perhaps the most provocative of these four parables. It is the second of three parables that Luke uses to illustrate God's concern for sinners, the other two being the parable of the lost sheep (Luke 15:1-7) and the parable of the prodigal son (perhaps more aptly called the parable of the prodigal father; Luke 15:11-32).

Luke 15:8-10

The Parable of the Lost Coin. [8]"Or what woman having ten coins and losing one would not light a lamp and sweep the house, searching carefully until she finds it? [9]And when she does find it, she calls together her friends and neighbors and says to them, 'Rejoice with me because I have found the coin that I lost.' [10]In just the same way, I tell you, there will be rejoicing among the angels of God over one sinner who repents."

In this parable, God is compared to a woman who had ten drachmae, each roughly equivalent to the Roman denarius and thought to be equivalent to a day's pay for an unskilled laborer. Having lost one of the drachmae, she cleans her house very carefully and diligently until she finds it, and then she hosts a big party of female friends—the Greek word *philas* is feminine—to celebrate the finding of her lost drachma. The party probably cost her more than a drachma, but no matter. This is how God and the angels rejoice over finding and returning one lost sinner. Imagine God behaving like this woman, having so much joy over finding one lost soul that she ends up inviting everyone she knows to the party!

It may surprise us to read about a feminine image of God in the Gospels. But the Bible contains other feminine images of God as well. For example, the prophet Hosea describes God as a mother of little children (Hos 11:3-4) and as a mother bear protecting her young (Hos 13:8; see also Deut 32:18; Isa 49:15; 66:13; Ps 131:2). Deuteronomy describes God as a mother eagle hovering over her young (Deut 32:11-12), and Isaiah describes God as a woman in labor (Isa 42:14). Finally, in the New Testament, Jesus describes himself as a mother hen gathering her chicks (Matt 23:37; Luke 13:34).

Of course, all language about God is metaphor since God, as creator and benefactor of all creation, is beyond gender or ethnicity or religious and cultural practice. But having both masculine and feminine images of God can help us relate to a God who is intimately involved in our lives and gives dignity to all beings (Gen 1:26-27).

Female Ministers of the Early Church

While the women in the parables of Jesus are fictional, they speak to how the coming reign of God should be understood among persons of faith, even comparing God to a woman who cleans her house in search of what is lost. But let us not forget about other named and therefore actual women of the New Testament, about whom little is known beyond a brief mention of their roles in the ministries of the early church.

Priscilla

First, let us look at Prisca, who is often referred to by the diminutive "Priscilla." Her husband's name was Aquila, and because she is often named first among the pair, biblical scholars have suggested that she was of higher social status than her husband. This may have made it more likely for her to be allowed to take on a leadership role in the Christian community.

Priscilla and Aquila are mentioned four times in the New Testament. Like Paul, they were Jews of Asia Minor who believed Jesus was the Christ. Romans 16:3-4 indicates that they were co-workers with Paul and that they had taken considerable risks to help Paul when he was in trouble, perhaps during his imprisonment in Ephesus or when he was in Corinth. Paul writes:

Romans 16:3-5a

Paul's Greetings. ³Greet Prisca and Aquila, my co-workers in Christ Jesus, ⁴who risked their necks for my life, to whom not only I am grateful but also all the churches of the Gentiles; ⁵greet also the church at their house.

When Paul writes his letter to the Romans, Prisca and Aquila are living in Rome. However, in his First Letter to the Corinthians, which Paul wrote from Ephesus (see 1 Cor 16:8), we hear that this couple was in charge of a church community that met in their home, presumably also in Ephesus:

---

1 Corinthians 16:19

¹⁹The churches of Asia send you greetings. Aquila and Prisca together with the church at their house send you many greetings in the Lord.

These early Christian churches were called "house churches." Well-to-do members of the Christian community would make their homes available for worship and would also support the community financially. Ordinary Mediterranean houses were small, consisting of one or two rooms and a courtyard or atrium, but wealthy people's homes had many rooms and a much larger atrium that could hold a community of 50–75 people. Only in the mid-third to early fourth century CE did Christians begin to construct public buildings for worship. Before this time, women had more freedom to actively participate in the life of the church because the home was the domain of women. However, when the churches became more public, women's roles were restricted to what was accepted in the prevailing culture.

 The concept of small groups of Christians **gathering in homes** still exists today. Consider, for example, the Base Christian Communities that emerged in the 1960s in Latin America.

Priscilla and Aquila are also mentioned in Second Timothy, where, once again, Priscilla is mentioned first:

---

2 Timothy 4:19

¹⁹Greet Prisca and Aquila and the family of Onesiphorus.

Although attributed to Paul, most New Testament scholars agree that Second Timothy was probably written by one of Paul's followers sometime around 80 CE (Paul was martyred c. 62–64 CE). The fact that this author mentions this couple approximately twenty years after Paul's death suggests that their reputation endured well beyond Paul's lifetime.

The Second Letter to Timothy also briefly mentions **Eunice and Lois**, Timothy's mother and grandmother (1:5). The author, writing under the pseudonym of Paul, expresses his gratitude for Timothy, his faithful companion, especially for the sincerity of his faith, which is described as having "lived" in his female ancestors for two generations already. Perhaps you know someone who "lives in faith" and who has influenced your spiritual growth in a similar way.

The fourth mention of Priscilla and Aquila is found in the Acts of the Apostles, which was composed sometime after 70 CE by the same person who wrote the Gospel of Luke. Acts reads like a history, but it is different from modern histories, which depend on documented evidence to tell the story of persons and events. Ancient histories, by contrast, were more interested in providing the reader with dramatic and compelling stories about important persons and events and incorporating them into a coherent narrative, complete with speeches created by the author to convey the author's interpretation of historical persons and events.

Here is what the Acts of the Apostles tells us about Priscilla and Aquila:

Acts 18:1-3, 18, 24-26

Paul in Corinth. ¹After this [Paul] left Athens and went to Corinth. ²There he met a Jew named Aquila, a native of Pontus, who had recently come from Italy with his wife Priscilla because Claudius had ordered all the Jews to leave Rome. He went to visit them ³and, because he practiced the same trade, stayed with them and worked, for they were tentmakers by trade. . . . ¹⁸Paul remained for quite some time, and after saying farewell to the brothers he sailed for Syria, together with Priscilla and Aquila. At Cenchreae he had his hair cut be-

---

cause he had taken a vow. . . . ²⁴A Jew named Apollos, a native of Alexandria, an eloquent speaker, arrived in Ephesus. He was an authority on the scriptures. ²⁵He had been instructed in the Way of the Lord and, with ardent spirit, spoke and taught accurately about Jesus, although he knew only the baptism of John. ²⁶He began to speak boldly in the synagogue; but when Priscilla and Aquila heard him, they took him aside and explained to him the Way [of God] more accurately.

Although the biblical text is fairly straightforward, two things are worthy of note. First, Priscilla is described, along with her husband, as a tentmaker (Greek *skénopoios*, often used to describe people who manufacture small travel tents out of leather or cloth made from black goat hair or canvas). Paul first comes to stay at their home and then works in their business, suggesting that Priscilla and Aquila's business was in their home.

Second, Priscilla and her husband were refugees who moved from Pontus in the region of the Black Sea coast of modern-day Turkey to Italy and then were exiled along with other Jews and Jewish Christians who were deemed to be troublemakers by the Roman emperor Claudius. We do not know about other places they might have lived, but, according to the Acts of the Apostles, Paul meets them in Corinth.

Third, Priscilla and Aquila were catechists who took responsibility for further educating Apollos, a rhetorician from Alexandria, Egypt, in a fuller understanding of "the Way of the Lord" (18:25). In the Acts of the Apostles, Christians were initially called "followers of the Way," hence the reference to "the Way of the Lord" in this passage (see Acts 24:14; cf. 9:1-2; 19:9, 23; 22:4). Because Priscilla is named first in this husband-and-wife duo, some biblical scholars have suggested that she might have been the lead catechist. Apollos is also mentioned in Paul's First Letter to the Corinthians as a missionary who visited the Christians in Corinth (see 1 Cor 3:4-9).

Phoebe, Benefactor and Deacon from Cenchreae

Chapter 16 of Romans is Paul's attempt to establish rapport and assert his credibility to the Christian community in Rome, a community he had not yet visited in his travels. The first woman mentioned here is Phoebe. We are told that she is from Cenchreae, a port city located on the eastern edge of the Corinthian isthmus of Greece, approximately five miles from Corinth. Biblical scholars have suggested that Phoebe was tasked with delivering Paul's letter to the Christian community in Rome and that Romans 16:1-2 constitutes his letter of recommendation on her behalf:

Romans 16:1-2

Phoebe Commended. ¹I commend to you Phoebe our sister, who is [also] a minister of the church at Cenchreae, ²that you may receive her in the Lord in a manner worthy of the holy ones, and help her in whatever she may need from you, for she has been a benefactor to many and to me as well.

Paul calls Phoebe "a minister of the church at Cenchreae" and his "benefactor" (16:1-2). The Greek word *prostatis*, translated here as "benefactor," means "a woman set over others" or "a female guardian, protector, or patron." Since she has been identified as his patroness, we can assume that Phoebe is an independently wealthy woman who can disperse her resources in support of whomever she chooses. In other words, Phoebe provided for Paul's needs, and he therefore owed her gratitude for befriending him and supporting his work.

Paul also describes Phoebe with the Greek word *diakonos*. The NABRE translates *diakonos* here as "minister," though it can also mean "deacon." In fact, *diakonos* can be used to refer to a wide range of roles, from a table server to an ordained deacon of the church. However, because Phoebe is also described as a patroness or a woman set over others, and because Paul is appealing to the church in Rome to receive her hospitably with the status she deserves among "the holy ones" (i.e., the believers; 16:2), we can reasonably assume that Paul intends *diakonos* to mean more than a table server when

Paul gives Phoebe the letter to the Roman Christians; Julius Schnorr von Carolsfeld (1794–1872)

Lesson Six

applied to Phoebe. She has a position of esteem in the church at Cenchreae, and Paul holds her in a position of influence or even authority as pertaining to his own ministry. Taking all of this into account, the New Revised Standard Version (NRSV) translates Romans 16:1 in this way: "I commend to you our sister Phoebe, a deacon of the church at Cenchreae."

The main argument against calling Phoebe a deacon has been that the early church had not yet established the official role of deacons at this time. While this is correct to some extent, the same would have to be said of the deacons mentioned in the opening of Paul's letter to the Philippians, which was most likely written shortly before the letter to the Romans. Philippians 1:1 reads, "[T]o all the holy ones in Christ Jesus who are in Philippi, with the overseers and ministers" (NABRE) or "To all the saints in Christ Jesus who are in Philippi, with the bishops and deacons" (NRSV). Regardless of whether *bishop* and *deacon* were ordained positions in the first century CE, they were, in practice, positions of authority in the church at Philippi.

The First Letter of Timothy, written in Paul's name toward the end of the first century CE, describes the kind of person who could be accepted as a deacon of the church. In doing so, the author uses the phrase "Women, similarly" (1 Tim 3:11). Some biblical scholars and some Christian denominations argue that these women are wives of deacons. Others say these are female deacons. The Greek word *guné* can be translated as "woman" or "wife," but if the author intended the latter, the text would have read, "*Their* wives, similarly" (see the footnote to 1 Tim 3:11 in the NABRE, which is authorized by the US Conference of Catholic Bishops).

Our clearest evidence for the ordination of female deacons in the early church comes from the *Didascalia Apostolorum*, a document composed in the mid-third century CE, and from the *Apostolic Constitutions*, which is a revised and expanded version of the former, written in the late fourth century CE. According to these documents, although male and female deacons were to work as one under the authority of the bishop, the work of female deacons was

in service of women in the community: to care for the sick, to assist in the baptism of female converts by going down into the water with them and anointing them with the holy oils, and by instructing female converts in the faith. All of these activities were in keeping with the rules of social decorum and cultural practice at that time. The *Apostolic Constitutions* contains the earliest known prayers for the ordination of male and female deacons (VIII.17-20).

Other Female Ministers Known to Paul

We have already described what we know about Phoebe, one of Paul's supporters and a deacon of the church in Cenchreae (Rom 16:1-2), and Priscilla, who, with her husband Aquila, was one of Paul's co-workers in Christ Jesus (Rom 16:3-4). In the remainder of Romans 16, Paul provides us with a rich treasure trove of names of evangelists and ministers of early Christianity whom he knew in one way or another. Of the twenty-six people mentioned there, eight are women. Such a large percentage of women is significant, especially given the highly patriarchal culture of the time. In Paul's greeting below, the names of these eight women are highlighted in bold type:

Romans 16:5b-16

Greet my beloved Epaenetus, who was the first-fruits in Asia for Christ. ⁶Greet **Mary**, who has worked hard for you. ⁷Greet Andronicus and **Junia**, my relatives and my fellow prisoners; they are prominent among the apostles and they were in Christ before me. ⁸Greet Ampliatus, my beloved in the Lord. ⁹Greet Urbanus, our co-worker in Christ, and my beloved Stachys. ¹⁰Greet Apelles, who is approved in Christ. Greet those who belong to the family of Aristobulus. ¹¹Greet my relative Herodion. Greet those in the Lord who belong to the family of Narcissus. ¹²Greet those workers in the Lord, **Tryphaena** and **Tryphosa**. Greet the beloved **Persis**, who has worked hard in the Lord. ¹³Greet Rufus, chosen in the Lord, and **his mother** and mine. ¹⁴Greet Asyncritus, Phlegon, Hermes, Patrobas, Hermas, and the brothers who are with them. ¹⁵Greet Philologus, **Julia**, Nereus and **his sister**, and Olympas, and all the holy ones who are with them. ¹⁶Greet one another with a holy kiss. All the churches of Christ greet you.

We know very little about any of these women, but the ethnicities suggested by their names and the attributes Paul attaches to them give us some clues about their ministry roles. The first is **Mary**. Her name suggests that she is a Jewish woman, and Paul's description indicates that she had some sort of leadership role in the Roman Christian community. Likewise, **Tryphaena**, **Tryphosa**, and **Persis** are described as workers in the Lord. However, these names are Greek, suggesting that these women were immigrants from the east or perhaps slaves, former slaves, or descendants of slaves. In other words, ministry in the early church was diverse, not only in terms of gender, but also in terms of ethnicity and social status.

Another pair of names on Paul's list of greetings is **Junia** (feminine noun) and Andronicus. Most likely, Andronicus is Junia's husband or perhaps a sibling. Paul says of this pair that they were his kinfolk (not literally, but as an expression of their closeness) who became followers of Jesus before he did, that they had suffered for the faith—a badge of courage and commitment for any early Christian—and that they were considered "prominent among the apostles" (16:7). In the history of interpretation of Romans 16, much effort was put into reading Junia's name as *Junias* (masculine noun). After all, how could a woman be identified as prominent among the apostles? Allowing for the possibility of female apostles in the earliest decades of the church poses some interesting and challenging questions for Christians even today.

Two women on this list are known only by their family relationships. One is the **mother of Rufus.** Paul describes her as being a mother to him as well. Rufus is a Latin name, suggesting that Rufus and his mother were Jews who

lived in Rome and ministered in some way to the Christians living there. The other woman mentioned in relation to a family member is the **sister of Nereus**. Both Nereus and his sister were members of a house church in Rome. Nereus is also the name of a god of the sea in Greek mythology, which suggests that this Christian named Nereus was a slave or former slave, since it was common practice to give names deriving from Greek mythology to slaves in Rome.

Nothing is said about **Julia** apart from her name. The name is Gentile and may suggest that she belonged to an aristocratic Julian family (descendants of Julius Caesar). Alternatively, she might have been a freedwoman or descendant of a freed person of the Julian family (Peter Lampe, *From Paul to Valentinus: Christians at Rome in the First Two Centuries*).

Euodia and Syntyche, Co-workers in the Spread of the Gospel

In his letter to the Philippians, Paul writes about two women, Euodia and Syntyche, who ministered in this church that he founded perhaps as early as 50 CE:

> #### Philippians 4:2-3
> ²I urge Euodia and I urge Syntyche to come to a mutual understanding in the Lord. ³Yes, and I ask you also, my true yokemate, to help them, for they have struggled at my side in promoting the gospel, along with Clement and my other co-workers, whose names are in the book of life.

Philippi was a prominent city located in eastern Macedonia in the northern part of the Greek peninsula. Apparently, these two women had some sort of not-so-private dispute, and so Paul urges them "to be of the same mind in the Lord" (4:2, my translation). This phrase also appears in Philippians 2:2, where it refers to encouraging one another in Christ, showing compassion and sympathy, acting in humility toward one another, loving one another, and sharing in the same Spirit.

Paul does not tell us the nature of Euodia and Syntyche's struggle, nor does he indicate that they are leaders of a house church. Instead, they are described as having struggled alongside Paul in the work of the Gospel (4:3). They might have been patrons of Paul's work or even evangelists of the message about Jesus. Their Greek names suggest lower-class status, perhaps descending from slaves or freed persons. But being "of the same mind as Christ" means that everyone who is part of the faith community is due the highest form of respect because they are one in the Spirit.

Tabitha, Maker of Clothes for Widows

The Acts of the Apostles contains some interesting stories about women who were involved in the activities of the early church. We will look at two of these women: Tabitha (Acts 9:36-42) and Lydia (Acts 16:11-15, 40). Remember that although Acts reads like a history, it is different from modern histories, which have much more written, documented evidence to rely upon than ancient writers had when composing their stories of important persons and events. A well-written ancient history engaged its readers with a clear narrative that tied together dramatic episodes that caught the "flavor" of its historical characters and with speeches that were penned by the author rather than literally spoken by the character. So, although the details of these stories are not based on additional historical documentation, we can still be fairly certain that both Tabitha and Lydia were historical persons.

In the scene that precedes Tabitha's story, the reader is told that Peter was in the area, making visits to the Christian communities in Judea, Galilee, and Samaria. While in Lydda, Peter heals a man who had been bedridden for eight years by saying, "Aeneas, Jesus Christ heals you. Get up and make your bed" (Acts 9:34). Immediately, he was healed. We are then told that those who lived in Lydda and the surrounding area heard about this and "turned to the Lord" (Acts 9:35). A dramatic episode, indeed! Lydda was located in central Israel on the Plain of Sharon. But nearby in Joppa, approximately ten miles to the northwest on the Mediterranean coast, Tabitha's friends and neighbors were dealing with her death:

Acts 9:36-41

Peter Restores Tabitha to Life. [36]Now in Joppa there was a disciple named Tabitha (which translated means Dorcas). She was completely occupied with good deeds and almsgiving. [37]Now during those days she fell sick and died, so after washing her, they laid [her] out in a room upstairs. [38]Since Lydda was near Joppa, the disciples, hearing that Peter was there, sent two men to him with the request, "Please come to us without delay." [39]So Peter got up and went with them. When he arrived, they took him to the room upstairs where all the widows came to him weeping and showing him the tunics and cloaks that Dorcas had made while she was with them. [40]Peter sent them all out and knelt down and prayed. Then he turned to her body and said, "Tabitha, rise up." She opened her eyes, saw Peter, and sat up. [41]He gave her his hand and raised her up, and when he had called the holy ones and the widows, he presented her alive.

Tabitha is not mentioned anywhere else in the New Testament. She is described with the Greek term *mathetria*, the feminine form of *mathétés*, meaning "disciple." This feminine form of "disciple" is found only here in the New Testament, though we know that the Gospels speak of other female disciples of Jesus (e.g., Luke 8:1-3). Tabitha's name is either Hebrew or Aramaic, and it translates as "Dorcas" in Greek. From this we can deduce that Tabitha was a Greek-speaking Jew. Because there is no mention of a husband, and because she is described as "full of good works and alms that she did continually" (Acts 9:36, my translation), we can also assume that she was a wealthy widow who could dispose of her resources as she chose.

When Tabitha died, members of the house church in Joppa knew that Peter was in the area, so two men were sent to fetch Peter and ask him to come without delay. Not every woman who suddenly gets sick and dies would warrant a visit from someone like Peter, so perhaps Tabitha was one of the patrons of this church.

Women were usually the ones who washed the body of the deceased and prepared it for burial. They also served as mourners for the funeral. Here we are told that the widows who had benefited from Tabitha's generosity were attending to her body when Peter arrives. Like the preceding healing, this resuscitation happens quickly and with dramatic effect. Peter sends everyone out of the room, calls Tabitha by name, and tells her to "rise up" (9:40). The narrator of the story does not tell us whether Peter knew Tabitha personally, but imagine Tabitha's surprise when she opened her eyes and saw an unrelated male in her bedroom!

The story about Tabitha's resuscitation raises an interesting question about the role of widows in the early church. Acts 6:1-6 describes how Jewish widows of the early Christian community, presumably in Jerusalem, were being neglected in the daily distribution of food. Luke does not tell us whether they had any ministry role; rather, they were the recipients of charity. The author of the First Letter to Timothy, written some thirty years later, tells us more about the qualifications of "true" widows—that is, elderly widows who had no children or grandchildren to support them. Apparently, these women could be enrolled to receive support from the faith community provided they had a reputation for good works, had raised their children well, and practiced hospitality. Also, they could *not* be idlers or gossips. Instead, they were to be continually engaged in prayer on behalf of the faith community (1 Tim 5:3-16).

Early Christianity, which had its roots in Judaism, may have also inherited the command to care for the widow and orphan (Exod 22:21-24; Deut 27:19; Zech 7:10; Ps 146:9) and, as a result, may have developed the practice of providing financial support to widows quite early in the church's history. However, the *Didascalia Apostolorum*, usually assigned a date of 250 CE, devotes two full chapters to an elaboration of the teaching on "true" widows from the First Letter to Timothy, with considerable attention given to the real or imagined misbehavior of women who had been enrolled in the order of widows. Apparently, some widows were earning extra money by teaching, and others were soliciting additional donations from individuals in the community to support their quality of life.

 Rhoda

Sometimes difficult situations call for a bit of comic relief, even in the Bible! The Acts of the Apostles tells the story of a servant named Rhoda who works in the home of Mary, the mother of John Mark (Acts 12:6-19). The people who are gathered at her house know that Peter is being held in prison under extremely tight security. Perhaps they also know that he is going to trial under Herod Agrippa the following morning.

That night, after he is miraculously freed from prison, Peter knocks on the gateway door to Mary's house. When Rhoda goes to the gate, she recognizes Peter's voice, but she is so excited that she runs to tell the others, leaving poor Peter standing outside! The people inside the home refuse to believe that Peter is free and alive, until they finally go to see who is still knocking on the gate. Rhoda is vindicated! Can you imagine the smile on her face?

Against this entrepreneurial activity, the *Didascalia* describes the widow as the "altar of God" who should sit at home, just as God's altar is fixed in one place, and pray day and night. There is nothing more that she needs to do. Rather than taking advantage of opportunities to earn more money, she should behave like the poor widow whom Jesus exalted above the Jewish religious authorities because she deposited everything she had—two small coins—in the temple treasury (Mark 12:41-44; Luke 21:1-4; *Didascalia Apostolorum* XV.3.6).

Of course, this is not the way we think of widows today at all. What if we were to reestablish the order of widows today? What might it look like?

Lydia, a Jewish Proselyte Who Becomes Head of a House Church

Another woman we meet in the Acts of the Apostles is Lydia. Her story is part of a longer section of Acts that describes Paul's ministry in and around Philippi (16:11-40). Philippi was a Roman colony located on the Egnatian Way, a Roman road that stretched from Istanbul, Turkey, to Durres (on the western shore of Albania). The narrator of the story notes that it was the leading city of Macedonia at the time (16:12).

Acts 16:13-15, 40

¹³On the sabbath we went outside the city gate along the river where we thought there would be a place of prayer. We sat and spoke with the women who had gathered there. ¹⁴One of them, a woman named Lydia, a dealer in purple cloth, from the city of Thyatira, a worshiper of God, listened, and the Lord opened her heart to pay attention to what Paul was saying. ¹⁵After she and her household had been baptized, she offered us an invitation, "If you consider me a believer in the Lord, come and stay at my home," and she prevailed on us. . . . ⁴⁰When [Paul and Silas] had come out of the prison, they went to Lydia's house where they saw and encouraged the brothers, and then they left.

We learn a great deal about Lydia in the space of a single verse of text (16:14). She is from Thyatira, located in what is now the western part of Turkey. In the first century, Thyatira was known for the production of purple-dyed cloth and for its wool workers, dyers, and clothing makers. The city's name is thought to be Lydian—that is, originating in the Lydian language of the region of western Turkey called Lydia. Likewise, Lydia may have received her name from the region of her birth. Lydia is described as a "worshiper of God," a synonym for another phrase, "God-fearing," that Luke frequently uses to refer to Gentiles who studied and worshiped with Jews but who did not fully convert to Judaism (e.g., Acts 10:2; 13:16).

Lydia is also described as a dealer or seller of purple cloth and dyes. Since she owned a home large enough to host guests (16:15), Lydia must have been fairly wealthy, but because working with dyed materials meant coming into contact with urine (commonly used as a dye fixative), she probably was not a member of an elite family. Shall we call her part of the *nouveau riche* of her time?

 The best of **purple dyes** was made from the liquid extracted from the tiny mucus sac of a murex, a carnivorous marine mollusk. It is estimated that it took 60,000 murex mollusks to make a pound of purple dye. Because the dye itself was very expensive, purple fabrics were available only to royalty and other extremely wealthy members of society.

How did Paul meet Lydia? While staying in Philippi, he inquired about a place to pray on the Sabbath. Remember that Paul was an observant Jew who never stopped being a Jew when he became a Jesus follower. Apparently, Philippi did not have an established synagogue. Hence, Paul and his fellow travelers needed to find a place near water that could be used for the ablutions before praying. Their investigation led them to a body of

"Procession of Women," a portion of a fresco remaining in one of the earliest known churches (Dura Europos, Syria, c. 233-256 CE), depicting either the women who come to complete the burial rituals of Jesus or the parable of the ten virgins. Provided by Yale-French Excavations at Dura-Europos.

water just outside the city, probably the creek called Crenides, about one-fifth of a mile west of the city. When they arrived, they found some women already gathered for prayer, so they sat and talked with them. Given the cultural expectation that men and women be separated in public spaces, Paul and his colleagues could have been seen as invading the women's space. Certainly, some of the women would have been offended and others fearful, even wanting to run away. But Lydia listened, we are told, and "the Lord thoroughly opened her heart to turn the mind toward the things being spoken by Paul" (16:14, my translation).

Immediately after hearing Paul's words, Lydia and her entire household were baptized. The baptism of an entire family and its servants might sound strange to those of us who live in a modern individualist culture, but it was common practice in collectivist cultures, where the goal was to promote the common good by acting in harmony with others. After the group baptism, we are told that Lydia did what a collectivist culture would expect: she offered hospitality to Paul and his colleagues in her home. Later, at the end of this section of Acts, it appears that Lydia also provided her home as a

place for the house church to meet (16:40). Thus, we can safely presume that Lydia, a woman of independent means, once a Gentile proselyte to Judaism and now a Christian, was the patroness of this house church. Was she also its leader?

Conclusion

We have come to the end of our study of the women of the New Testament, but hopefully this will not be the end of our reflection on their lives as models of faith, service, and leadership among the followers of Jesus. I hope knowing more about the world in which these women lived—their communitarian culture, the biases and challenges they faced—has made their stories more compelling for you. Together, may we draw sustenance from Mary the mother of Jesus, the Samaritan woman, Martha and Mary, Mary Magdalene, the women healed by Jesus, and all the women who participated in the ministry of the early church. May we have courage to model our lives after theirs as we search out our own spiritual paths as followers of Jesus in today's world.

EXPLORING LESSON SIX

1. The commentary offers one definition of what a parable is. Explain in your own words what makes a parable different from a story that is not a parable.

_____

_____

_____

_____

_____

2. Among the four Gospel parables that have a woman as a central character, which is your favorite and why? Which, if any, is most troubling or puzzling to you?

_____

_____

_____

_____

_____

3. The New Testament contains several references to Priscilla and Aquila, whom Paul called "co-workers in Christ Jesus" (Rom 16:3) and leaders of a "church at their house" (Rom 16:5; 1 Cor 16:19). What aspects of their story are new or surprising to you? If it would be possible to interview her today, what else would you like to know about Priscilla?

_____

_____

_____

_____

_____

4. Phoebe is mentioned only once in the New Testament, but apparently she had an important role in the house church at Cenchreae. Paul calls her a minister (Greek *diakonos*) of that church and one of his valued benefactors (Rom 16:1-2). Using what you know about women in the early church and what Paul says about her, how might you describe Phoebe's attributes and accomplishments? What do you value most about her? Does she remind you of anyone in your own life or faith community?

_____

_____

_____

_____

_____

5. In Romans 16, Paul mentions several women who are involved in the ministries of the early church as a way of offering a letter of recommendation for himself to the church at Rome, a community that had not yet met him. The female names are listed in bold font in the commentary. What does Romans 16 suggest to you about the role of women in the life of the early church?

_____

_____

_____

_____

_____

_____

6. Tabitha is another first-century female church member who is mentioned only once in the New Testament (Acts 9:36-41). Using what you know about women in the early church and what the author of the Acts of the Apostles says about her, how would you describe Tabitha in your own words? What do you value most about her? Does she remind you of anyone you know and appreciate?

_____

_____

_____

_____

_____

_____

_____

7. The Acts of the Apostles also includes a story about Lydia, a trader in purple cloth, and a head of a house church in Philippi (Acts 16:11-40). Using what you know about women in the early church and what the author of the Acts of the Apostles says about her, how would you describe Lydia's attributes and accomplishments? What do you value most about her? Does she remind you of anyone?

_____

_____

_____

_____

_____

_____

_____

8. As indicated in the commentary, some of the features of church communities in the late first and early second centuries included house churches led by women, female deacons who assisted male deacons in service of women's needs, and widows who were enrolled as prayer partners for their respective communities. Church structures and organizations can vary based on the needs of the church in a particular place and time. What might be the advantages and disadvantages of having women serving in leadership positions in the church, of ordaining female deacons, and/or reestablishing the order of widows (or some other related order) among our Christian communities today?

---

9. Reflect on one or two things that will stay with you from this experience of studying women in the New Testament. Which women did you find most interesting? What did you most enjoy learning about? What did you struggle with? How will this study impact you going forward?

CLOSING PRAYER

Prayer

*I commend to you Phoebe our sister, who is
[also] a minister of the church at Cenchreae,
that you may receive her in the Lord in a
manner worthy of the holy ones . . .*

(Romans 16:1-2)

Gracious and loving God, we thank you for the witness
of Phoebe and Priscilla, Tabitha and Lydia, and the
many other women of the New Testament who set the
foundation for female ministries in the early church,
serving as apostles, co-workers in Paul's ministry, heads
of house churches, deaconesses, and widows. You
inspired Paul to say to the churches of Galatia, "There
is neither Jew nor Greek, there is neither slave nor free
person, there is not male and female; for you are all one
in Christ Jesus" (Gal 3:28). May the same be true for our
generation, that all of us may embrace our God-given
and Spirit-infused gifts for the good of your holy church.
Inspired by all these women of God, and in gratitude
for our time of prayer and study together, we pray today
especially for . . .

FOR FURTHER INVESTIGATION

Lesson One: Mary, Mother of Jesus

If you are interested in a theological reflection on the life of Mary, the mother of Jesus, please consider Elizabeth Johnson's *Dangerous Memories: A Mosaic of Mary in Scripture* (New York/London: Continuum, 2004).

If you are interested in exploring the role of Mary, the mother of Jesus, in doctrine and practice over the centuries, you might want to read Jaroslav Pelikan's *Mary Through the Centuries: Her Place in the History of Culture* (New Haven/London: Yale University Press, 1996).

For those who are interested in other early traditions about Mary, the mother of Jesus, you may wish to explore the noncanonical (not included in the Bible) *Infancy Gospel of James*, also known as the *Protevangelium of James*. Originally written in Greek and dating to the mid-second century CE, it was first attributed to James, the brother of the Lord, though we do not know the identity of its author. Although not actual history, the *Infancy Gospel of James* addresses some important theological questions that were circulating in early church communities, like why Mary was chosen to be the mother of Jesus, how she became married to Joseph, and how it was that Jesus could have had brothers if Mary was perpetually a virgin. The *Infancy Gospel of James* was widely read in the early centuries of the church and is available today in a fresh English translation by Lily Vuong, entitled *The Protevangelium of James* (Eugene, OR: Cascade Books, 2019). Earlier translations can be found at https://www.earlychristianwritings.com/infancyjames.html.

Lesson Two: Women Beneficiaries of Jesus' Miracles

If you wish to explore the topic of Jesus' miracle-working in more detail, consider reading Amy-Jill Levine's *Signs and Wonders: A Beginner's Guide to the Miracles of Jesus* (Nashville: Abingdon Press, 2022).

For the social and cultural background to Jesus' miracle-working and other aspects of the Gospels, these resources are particularly helpful:

Malina, Bruce, and Richard Rohrbaugh. *Social-Science Commentary on the Gospel of John*. Minneapolis: Fortress Press, 1998.

Malina, Bruce, and Richard Rohrbaugh. *Social-Science Commentary on the Synoptic Gospels*. 2nd ed. Minneapolis: Fortress Press, 2003.

Pilch, John J. *Healing in the New Testament: Insights from Medical and Mediterranean Anthropology*. Minneapolis: Fortress Press, 2000.

Lesson Three: The Samaritan Woman of John's Gospel

There are almost as many interpretations of the story of the Samaritan woman at the well as there are biblical scholars who study it, but one you might especially enjoy is by Jewish scholar Eli Lizorkin-Eyzenberg, who wrote *The Samaritan Woman Reconsidered* (Jewish Studies for Christians, 2019). His reflections can help us understand this story as our Jewish brothers and sisters might interpret it.

Lesson Four: Mary and Martha, Models of Devotion and Service

If you would like to explore the stories of Mary and Martha in greater detail, you might like to read Satoko Yamaguchi's *Mary & Martha: Women in the World of Jesus* (Maryknoll, NY: Orbis Press, 2002).

The story of Jesus visiting Mary and Martha at their home (Luke 10:38-42) was a popular topic for sixteenth-century European artists. You might wish to investigate two paintings from that period—*Christ in the House of Martha and Mary* by Johannes Vermeer and *Jesus in the House of Martha and Mary* by Erasmus Quellinus II and Adriaen van Utrecht—to see how they interpret this Gospel story. A simple internet search will bring up several photos of these works of art. Pay special attention to the way perspective, color, and placement of the central characters are used. What does the characters' body language convey about their dispositions? What aspects of the paintings are consistent with the biblical story, and where do the artists add their own interpretation of the scene?

Lesson Five: Mary Magdalene, Apostle of the Resurrection

If you would like to explore this topic further, there are several excellent academic studies on Mary Magdalene, including the following:

> Haskins, Susan. *Mary Magdalen: Myth and Metaphor*. New ed. London: Random House, 2007.

> Schaberg, Jane. *The Resurrection of Mary Magdalene: Legends, Apocrypha, and the Christian Testament*. New York/London: Continuum, 2002.

If you would like to read and learn more about the second-century Gnostic *Gospel of Mary Magdalene*, Karen King has written an introduction and modern English translation under the title *The Gospel of Mary of Magdala: Jesus and the First Woman Apostle* (Santa Rosa, CA: Polebridge Press, 2003).

You might also want to explore the *Golden Legend*, which is a collection of legends of the saints put together by Jacobus de Voragine (c. 1228–96), a Dominican priest and archbishop of Genoa, to be used as readings throughout the church year. A modern translation by William Granger Ryan entitled *The Golden Legend: Readings of the Saints* is available through Princeton University Press (reprint ed., 2012). A translation by William Caxton of chapter 96 of the *Golden Legend*, which contains the stories associated with Mary Magdalene, can also be found at https://www.christianiconography.info /goldenLegend/magdalene.htm.

Lesson Six: Other Important But Lesser-Known Women of the New Testament

If you are interested in digging more deeply into the history of women's ministry in the early church, consider the following academic studies:

> Lee, Dorothy A. *The Ministry of Women in the New Testament: Reclaiming the Biblical Vision for Church Leadership*. Grand Rapids: Baker Academic, 2021.

> Madigan, Kevin, and Caroline Osiek, eds. and trans. *Ordained Women in the Early Church: A Documentary History*. 1st ed. Baltimore: Johns Hopkins University Press, 2011.

You might also like to read the full text of the *Didascalia Apostolorum* to learn more about the qualifications and responsibilities of leadership positions in the early church (https://www.earlychristianwritings.com/text/didascalia .html). The full text of the *Apostolic Constitutions* is also easily accessible (https://www.newadvent.org/fathers/07158.htm).

Regarding modern questions of church leadership, you might be interested in Pope St. John Paul II's apostolic letter entitled *Ordinatio Sacerdotalis: On Reserving Priestly Ordination to Men Alone* (https://www.vatican .va/content/john-paul-ii/en/apost_letters/1994/documents/hf_jp-ii_apl _19940522_ordinatio-sacerdotalis.html).

You might also find the following resources to be helpful:

> Macy, Gary, William T. Ditewig, and Phyllis Zagano. *Women Deacons: Past, Present, Future*. New York/Mahwah, NJ: Paulist Press, 2012.

> Zagano, Phyllis. *Women: Icons of Christ*. New York/Mahwah, NJ: Paulist Press, 2020.

PRAYING WITH YOUR GROUP

Because we know that the Bible allows us to hear God's voice, prayer provides the context for our study and sharing. By speaking and listening to God and each other, the discussion often grows to more deeply bond us to one another and to God.

At *the beginning and end of each lesson* simple prayers are provided for individual use, and also may be used within the group setting. Most of the closing prayers provided with each lesson relate directly to a theme from that lesson and encourage you to pray together for people and events in your local community.

Of course, there are many ways to center ourselves in God's presence as we gather together in groups around the word of God. We provide some additional suggestions here knowing you and your group will make prayer a priority as part of your gathering. These are simply alternative ways to pray if your group would like to try something different from those prayers provided in the previous pages.

Conversational Prayer

This form of prayer allows for the group members to pray in their own words in a way that is not intimidating. The group leader begins with Step One, inviting all to focus on the presence of Christ among them. After a few moments of quiet, the group leader invites anyone in the group to voice a prayer or two of thanksgiving; once that is complete, then anyone who has personal intentions may pray in their own words for their needs; finally, the group prays for the needs of others.

A suggested process:
In your own words, speak simple and short prayers to allow time for others to add their voices.

Focus on one "step" at a time, not worrying about praying for everything in your mental list at once.

Step One	Visualize Christ. Welcome him.
	Imagine him present with you in your group.
	Allow time for some silence.
Step Two	Gratitude opens our hearts.
	Use simple words such as, "Thank you, Lord, for . . ."
Step Three	Pray for your own needs knowing that others will pray with you.
	Be specific and honest.
	Use "I" and "me" language.

Step Four	Pray for others by name, with love.
	You may voice your agreement ("Yes, Lord").
	End with gratitude for sharing concerns.

Praying Like Ignatius

St. Ignatius Loyola, whose life and ministry are the foundation of the Jesuit community, invites us to enter into Scripture texts in order to experience the scenes, especially scenes of the gospels or other narrative parts of Scripture. Simply put, this is a method of creatively imagining the scene, viewing it from the inside, and asking God to meet you there. Most often, this is a personal form of prayer, but in a group setting, some of its elements can be helpful if you allow time for this process.

A suggested process:

- Select a scene from the chapters in the particular lesson.
- Read that scene out loud in the group, followed by some quiet time.
- Ask group members to place themselves in the scene (as a character, or as an onlooker) so that they can imagine the emotions, responses, and thinking that may have taken place. Notice the details and the tone, and imagine the interaction with the Lord that is taking place.
- Share with the group any insights that came to you in this quiet imagining.
- Allow each person in the group to thank God for some insight and to pray about some request that may have surfaced.

Sacred Reading (or Lectio Divina)

This method of prayer invites us to "listen with the ear of the heart" as St. Benedict's rule would say. We listen to the words and the phrasing, asking God to speak to our innermost being. Again, this method of prayer is most often used in an individual setting but may also be used in an adapted way within a group.

A suggested process:

- Select a scene from the chapters in the particular lesson.
- Read the scene out loud in the group, perhaps two times.
- Ask group members to ponder a word or phrase that stands out to them.
- The group members could then simply speak the word or phrase as a kind of litany of what was meaningful for your group.
- Allow time for more silence to ponder the words that were heard, asking God to reveal to you what message you are meant to hear, how God is speaking to you.
- Follow up with spoken intentions at the close of this group time.

REFLECTING ON SCRIPTURE

Reading Scripture is an opportunity not simply to learn new information but to listen to God who loves you. Pray that the same Holy Spirit who guided the formation of Scripture will inspire you to correctly understand what you read, and empower you to make what you read a part of your life.

The inspired word of God contains layers of meaning. As you make your way through passages of Scripture, whether studying a book of the Bible or focusing on a biblical theme, you may find it helpful to ask yourself these four questions:

What does the Scripture passage say?
Read the passage slowly and reflectively. Become familiar with it. If the passage you are reading is a narrative, carefully observe the characters and the plot. Use your imagination to picture the scene or enter into it.

What does the Scripture passage mean?
Read the footnotes in your Bible and the commentary provided to help you understand what the sacred writers intended and what God wants to communicate by means of their words.

What does the Scripture passage mean to me?
Meditate on the passage. God's word is living and powerful. What is God saying to you? How does the Scripture passage apply to your life today?

What am I going to do about it?
Try to discover how God may be challenging you in this passage. An encounter with God contains a challenge to know God's will and follow it more closely in daily life. Ask the Holy Spirit to inspire not only your mind but your life with this living word.